PENCIL DRAWING
STILL LIFE
Book One

CHARCOAL DRAWING
Understanding and Applying Values
Shading Solid Objects
Applying Light to Landscapes
Creating Form with Human Faces and Body

PEN, BRUSH AND INK DRAWING
SKETCHING LANDSCAPE AND CITYSCAPE
Book Three

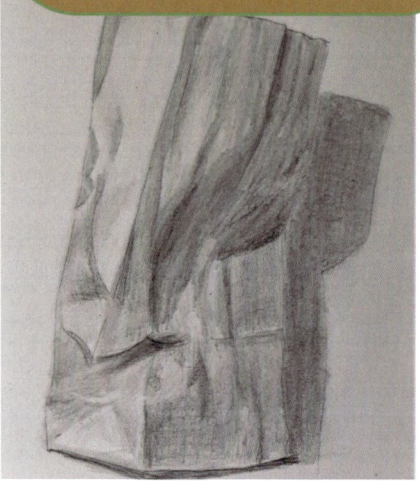

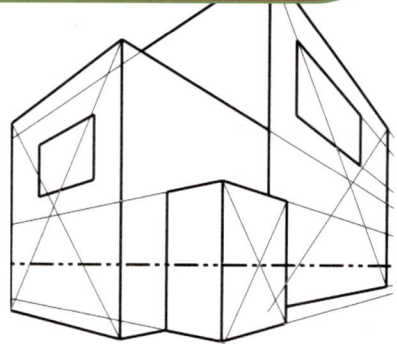

TWO POINT PERSPECTIVE

PENCIL DRAWING
Simple Geometric Shapes
Turning 2-D to 3-D
Drapery and Wrinkles
Patterns and Textures
Applying Still Life in Other Artworks

CHARCOAL DRAWING
FORM AND SHADING
Book Two

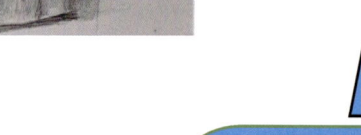

PEN, BRUSH AND INK DRAWING
Sketching Landscape, Cityscape and Seascape
Applying Perspective
Drawing Cartoons
Drawing with Ink and Wash
Working with Scratch Board

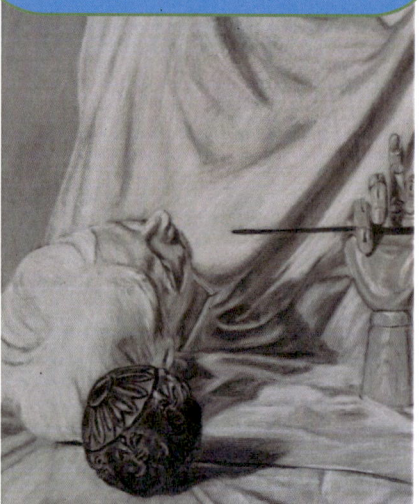

PASTELS DRAWING
PORTRAITS
Book Five

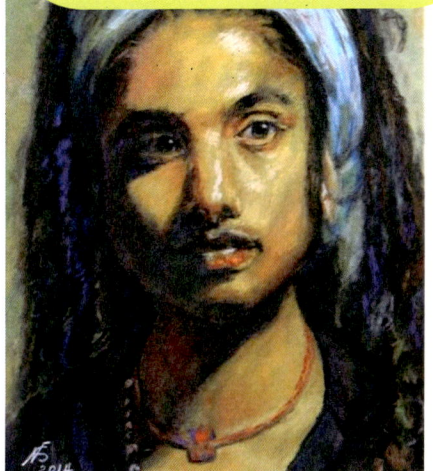

COLOR PENCILS DRAWING

Understanding Colors
Selecting and Working with Various Papers
Creating Textures of Various Animals and Nature

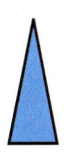

PRINCIPLES OF DESIGN

Understanding and Creating Exceptional Compositions
Creating Better Drawings

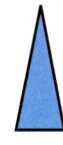

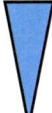

COLOR PENCILS DRAWING
NATURE/WILDLIFE
Book Four

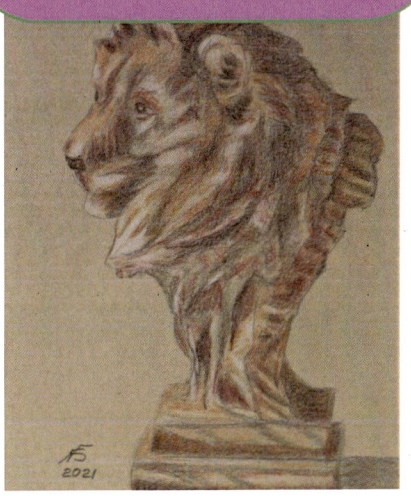

PASTELS DRAWING

Understanding the Emotion of Color
Working with Still Life
Working with Landscapes
Working with Animals and Portraitures

APPLYING THE PRINCIPLES AND ELEMENTS OF ART
Book Six

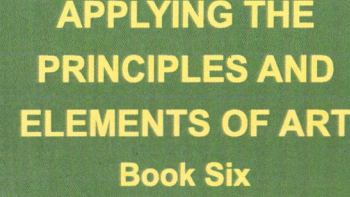

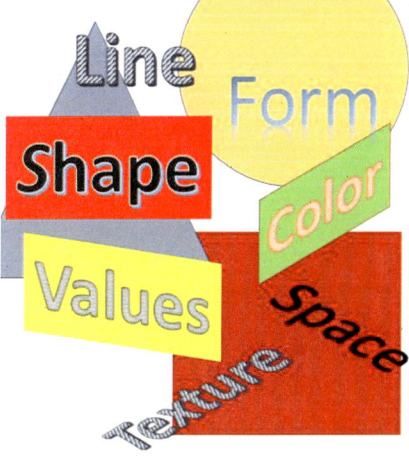

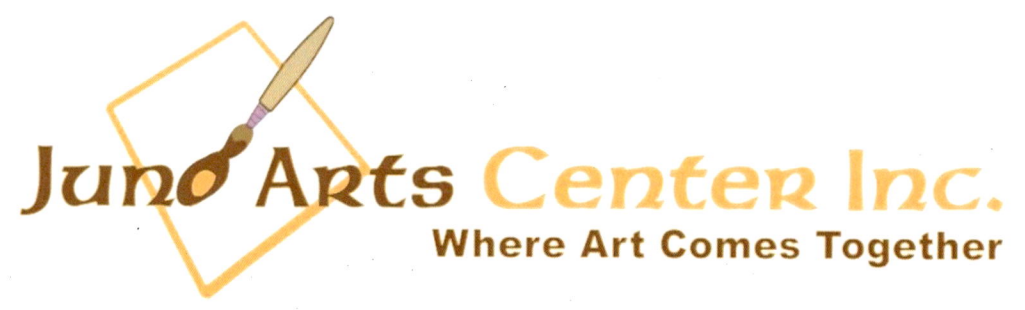

Norman F. Simms, MFA
Introduction to Drawing Series
Book Two

CHARCOAL DRAWING
FORM AND SHADING

SIMPLE GEOMETRIC SHAPES
TURNING 2-D TO 3-D
DRAPERY AND WRINKLES
PATTERNS AND TEXTURES
APPLYING STILL LIFE IN OTHER ARTWORKS

Acknowledgments

The author would like to acknowledge all the people who encouraged him to pursue his dream in becoming and working as an artist. He wants to give thanks to his parents, Leon E. Simms, Senior and Ethel S. Simms, for enrolling him in his first art school years ago when he was attending junior high school in Washington, D.C.

He wants to thank his wife, Dawn Chism Simms, for encouraging him to continue to seek a career in art and for continuing to push him to create beauty through his artworks. She is also the backbone of editing his writing. She is a blessing and a friend and they work well together as a team.

He wants to thank all the artist associations and art students who confronted him with many questions of how to approach and understand artworks and who encouraged him to write his books on various art related subjects. He also wants to thank all the artists and art lovers who are reading and viewing this book.

He would like to give thanks to all of the professional artists (Christine Hanlon, Warren Chang, Jennie Brunnick, Jung Han Kim, Sean Connor, and John Poon) who have given him a strong foundation for understanding the powers and the mysteries behind great artworks.

Copyright @2021   by Norman F. Simms.

All rights reserved. No part of this book may be reproduced or transmitted in any form or by any means, electronic or mechanical, including photocopying, recording, or by any information storage and retrieval system, without permission in writing from the copyright owner.

These rights are waived for students learning and wanting to reproduce sections to learn or to use as reference for educational purposes.

All artworks and illustrations in this book are those of the author.

Norman F. Simms, MFA
Juno Arts Center Inc.
1-215-269-0390
normanfsimms@outlook.com
https://www.normanfinearts.com/

Autobiography

The artist, Norman Francis Simms, was born in Washington, DC in the year 1956. He graduated from his first art school, Art Instruction Schools, in 1975. He attended Murray State University on a track scholarship where he continued his education in fine arts. He changed his education path to study various Engineering topics at the Washington School for Drafting Technology and earned an Associate's Degree in Electrical Engineering Technology at its Center for Degree Studies. He later earned a Bachelor's Degree in Information Systems at the University of Maryland.

For many years, Norman worked for large engineering corporations creating engineering drawings and illustrations, but he felt he wanted to express himself beyond the commercial arena. His passion for his first love - art - became too strong to ignore. He finally attended the Academy of Art located in San Francisco, California earning a Master's Degree in Fine Arts.

Norman creates dynamic paintings and drawings of various mediums and has exhibited his artworks regionally in solo and group exhibitions in Maryland, Pennsylvania, New Jersey and New York City from the years 2002 to 2020. He has received the "Palmer Award for Excellence" at the Trenton City Museum at Ellarslie for his oil painting, "The Artist and his Model". His pastel paintings, "Butterfly Dance", "Reflection", and "Blossom", have been featured in *The Best of America Pastel Artists Volume II*. His oil painting, "The Artist and his Model", has also been published in the book, *Important World Artists Vol. I, A World of Art*.

He currently teaches various Fine Art classes on painting and drawing, live online and face-to-face, at several campuses of Bucks County Community College in Pennsylvania.

He is also a member of the national fine arts organizations, *Portrait Society of America*, *The Pastel Society of America*, and *Oil Painters of America*, and the local arts organizations in Bucks County, *Artsbridge*, *Artists of Yardley,* and *Artists of Bristol on the Delaware*. He has published two books on art-related topics - *Portrait and Nude Painting*

& *Philosophies* (2012) and *Interview between the Jackass and the Artist* (2013, Revised 2021), and is working on several other books on other art-related topics.

He is the CEO and Founder of Juno Arts Center Inc., a Pennsylvania corporation that produces and sells original artworks of its Founder, fine artwork prints, and art-related books. Copies of many of his original oil and pastel paintings and charcoal and pencil drawings are displayed in an online gallery at the website, https://www.normanfinearts.com/.

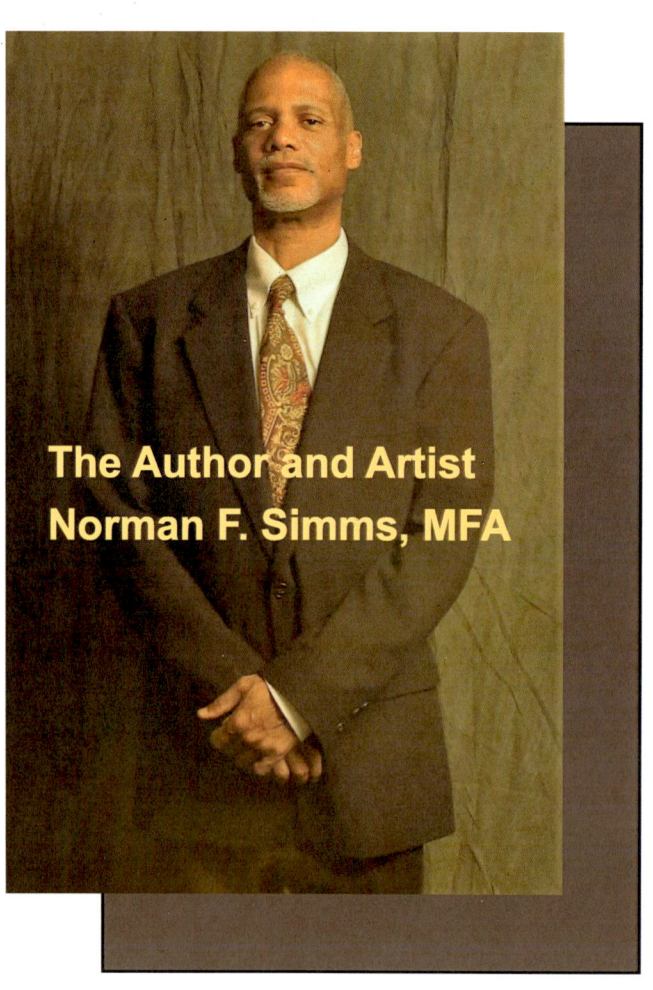

The Author and Artist
Norman F. Simms, MFA

Preface

I feel that it is imperative for artists to continue exploring new ways to see and communicate ideas, to educate and expose the world to new beauties and viewpoints. Our job as artists is to entertain and enlighten our viewers. If you are like me and want to deliver a universal message, a message that states that life is a beautiful thing despite the bumps and unexpected twists we go through during life's journey, you will enjoy expanding that beauty by adding your creative drawings in a way that only you can. This is the purpose for writing this book. It is for you to achieve success, happiness, and joy in learning how to draw and create your own wonderful drawings.

Why We Draw?

We draw to stimulate our minds, as we must focus on planning, reasoning, movement, emotion and problem solving, whether it is a technical drawing or a landscape in our neighborhood. You have to activate your mind's visual processing and work with your perception, observation, and memory. This mind exercise creates a feeling of calmness as your mind develops a keen sense of focus. Drawing involves exploring various subjects and topics, including one's self visually in and out of this world. Drawing is more than just copying the subject matter; it is interpreting what you see and visually communicating the ideas and feelings that you personally relate to – referred to as self-expression.

Drawing is visual thinking – a way of exploring and understanding ideas and experiences as we record people, places, things, memories and events. Drawing is a record of existence and varies from each individual as each individual has a different life and experience, which creates different types and styles of marks on flat surfaces.

Scope

This book will be exploring and working with values to create the illusion of form on 2-dimensional surfaces using the medium of charcoal. Charcoal can produce tones that are not only very light but also intensely black. Artists used charcoal to create preliminary studies to finished drawings. For this reason, drawing with charcoal is ideal for drawing portraits and figures, which will be covered in some detail in this book.

As you practice and get familiar with this medium, you will learn some general locations of features that are placed on the human face, as well as some features that are only located on parts of the human body, arms, and legs. You will practice on simplifying the human form, using shading, in order to create a more realistic representation of what you see.

To get good at drawing with charcoal or any medium for that matter, do a drawing every day. Redraw your drawings several times in different ways and from different viewpoints. Look at other drawings, from simple line drawings to meticulously detailed renderings. You will learn both from observation and doing (this means drawing from other drawings, photographs, and life.)

If you draw daily, you will need to keep a sketchbook. Try to improve your speed and coordination by working with various curves and shapes in drawings as a warm-up frequently. Use perspective, which will be covered in great detail in Book Three, and understand and improve by creating proportion within your drawing.
finally, most important, remember to have fun when you are drawing.

Learning to Draw

There are no right or wrong ways to draw, but after years of studies, I will approach drawing in a logical way, that will allow you to slowly build your technical, compositional and comprehensive skills. Remember that there are many ways to draw – as you visualize the world. You will learn to draw what you see and to draw conceptually. Some things I will not be able to teach, such as patience - try to take deep breaths, relax and enjoy the moment, feel free to make mistakes, experiment to expand your visual and drawing vocabulary. In completing this book and others in the series, you should:

• Think of the big picture rather than parts – work on the entire composition at the same time.

• Observe relationships between forms and all negative and positive spaces.

• Create a focal point by emphasizing some elements and deemphasizing others.

• Arrange the composition to guide the viewer through the pictorial journey of shapes and space.

• Create a work of fine art that you and others will enjoy looking at.

X

Understanding Drawing and How it is Taught

I would like to welcome you to drawing, a practice used to visually communicate concepts, ideas or emotions. Drawing is a combination of straight and/or curved lines that represent thought. This thought is able to express ideas, directions, feelings, or a combination of all of these visually.

There are three general categories of creating representative drawings: technical drawings, sometimes referred to as design drawings, physical observation/realistic or Atelier drawings, and imaginative drawings, where memory is extensively used.

Teaching Methods for Learning to Draw

Academy setting (workshop or studio) is where a professional artist (master) and his or her students are in the most ideal environment for the apprentices to grow as artists. This is because they receive instant feedback. The academy setting has become popular because it is presented in the form of standardized learning, additional tips, and learning from several sources. The academy setting is necessary due to larger numbers of students and the time constraints of both the student and the master.

Technical or design drawings consist of multi-view drawings; a related set of orthographic projections. Each projection reveals a particular aspect of an object. Together, they are able to fully describe the object in both 2-dimensional and 3-dimensional forms.

Orthographic projection uses views to project adjacent views perpendicular to the picture plane. These views are 2-dimensional. To create a sense of depth to 2-dimensional images, we need to know their height, width, and depth. In fine art, we use perspective and foreshortening to depict 3-dimensional subjects and distance.

Perspective is a technique for depicting volumes and relationships of depth on a flat surface. There are aerial, linear, and foreshortening perspectives. In technical drawings, linear perspective is used and assumes the viewer sees through a single eye. People with two eyes almost never see anything in this way. We constantly scan, collect, manipulate, and process data to form our perception and understanding of the visual world. Still linear perspective is a valuable tool and can give the observer the feel of a 3-dimensional world.

Technical drawings are created by measurement only. Their purpose is to have manufacturers, builders, or site planners use these drawings as an accurate guide to making components, products, architectural or site plans for laying out plans from these drawings. Today these drawings are usually done on a computer using CAD (Computer Aided Design) softwares.

Physical observation drawings are mental examinations of forms and shapes relationships. Art instructors will often hear the statement: "I can't draw". This statement is not totally true, but neither is it totally false. Masterful drawing is a combination of work and knowledge. You need to have a sound foundation of the fundamentals and draftsmanship or skill of drawing, without using any aids. Mastering the draftsmanship of drawing is like learning to add, subtract, and multiply, without using a calculator. When you can place a line exactly where you want it, and when you can draw a shape exactly as you see or choose to interpret it, then you have become skilled at drawing.

We use our eyes and brain to subconsciously see distorted realisms. This is the reason it is difficult for many to accurately draw. Drawing is problematic for some beginners, partly for the reason that everything we see is interpreted by the mind, and everyone's mind has some pre-established patterns of how things should look. In other words, we don't always really see what's in front of us. Nevertheless, we fall back on the images in our mind. People who have trouble drawing keep relying on these memorized pictures in their minds that prevent their eyes from seeing the true shapes, colors, and textures of things they draw.

Drawing is more than a mere representation of something before the viewer. It is a series of inviting or defensive marks. If you approach drawing not knowing the "why" behind the madness that dominates the viewer, then your skills are also lacking. Remember the general purpose of drawing is to communicate.

Even as a hobbyist, it is frustrating to rely on luck to communicate your thoughts, emotions, and energy to your viewers.

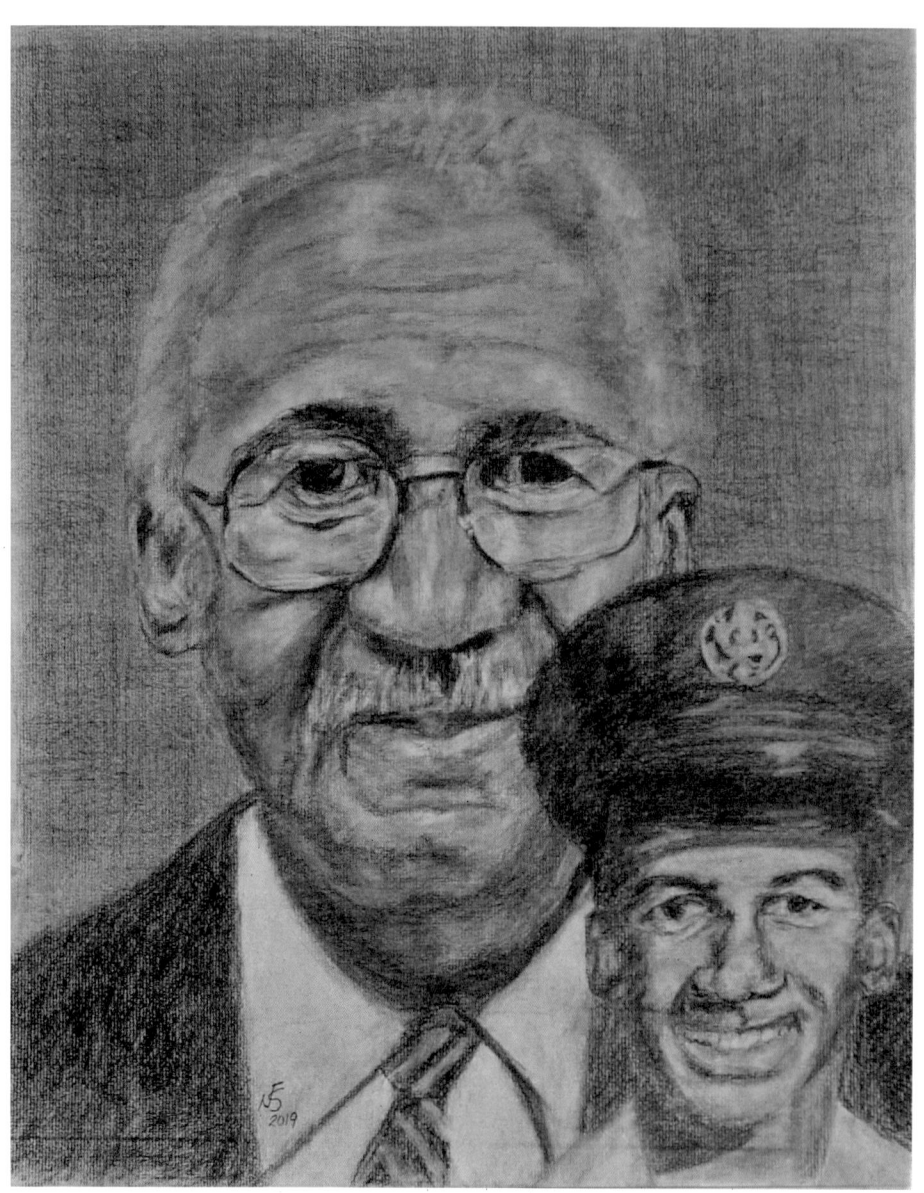

**Charcoal drawing on Charcoal Paper,
Young at Heart, 18" X 24"**

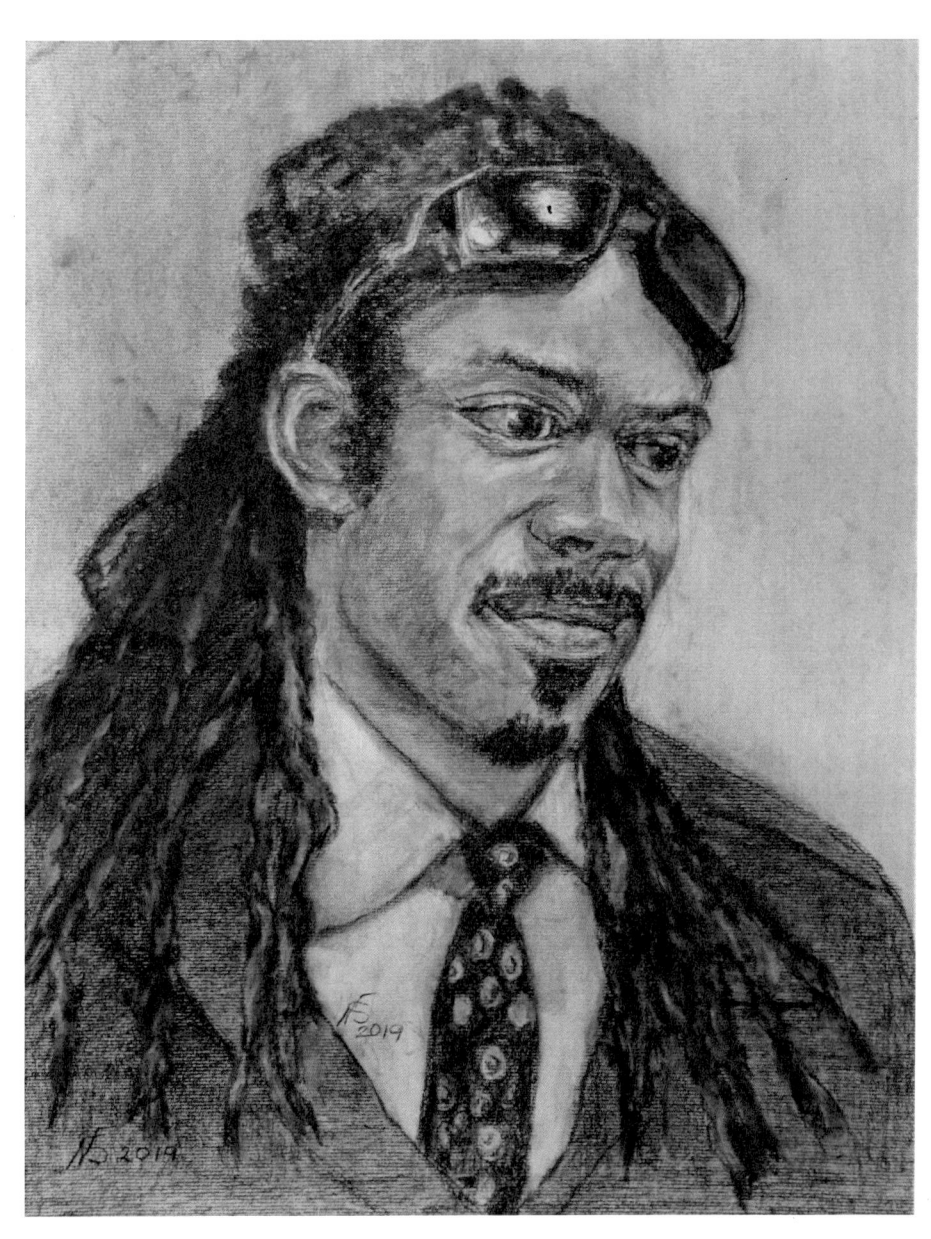

**Charcoal Drawing, on Charcoal Paper,
Dreadlocks and Sunglasses, 18" X 24"**

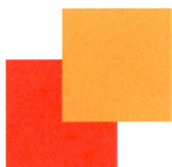

BOOK TWO
TABLE OF CONTENTS
CHARCOAL - Form and Shading

Lists of Introduction to Drawing Book Series	I
Acknowledgments	IV
Copyright Page	V
Autobiography	VI
Preface	VIII
Scope	IX
Learning to Draw	X
Understanding Drawing and How it is Taught	XI
Book Two - Table of Contents, Charcoal - Form and Shading	XV
Visual Communication as an Artist	1
Introduction to Charcoal Drawing	3
Charcoal Drawing	5
Tools and Materials for Drawing with Charcoal	6
Marking Tools for Charcoal Drawing	7
Charcoal Pencils	7
Willow or Vine Charcoal Sticks	8
Other Forms of Charcoal	8
Paper for Charcoal Drawing	9
Newsprint	9
Toned Paper	9
Fixative (Workable)	10
Final Notes on Paper	10
Shading	11
Light and Dark Values	12
Chiaroscuro Values for Solid Forms	13
Applying Light and Shadows	14
Assignment: BK 2-01 Shading on White Charcoal Paper	15
Assignment: BK 2-02 Shading on Gray Toned Paper	16
Quiz BK 2-01 (Shading)	17
Quiz BK 2-01 Answers	18

Facial Features Locations	19
Steps in Creating a Facial Template	21
Value Keys	25
Working with Landscape Artworks	26
Working with Landscape Artworks - Step by Step	27
Quiz BK 2-02 (Applying Values to Landscapes)	31
Quiz BK 2-02 Answers	32
The Art of Nudes	33
Understanding the Human Anatomy and Figure Drawing	34
Starting with the Stick Figures	35
The Spine	37
The Neck	38
The Upper Body	39
The Pelvis	40
The Head Mass, Cage Mass, and Pelvis Mass	41
Limbs (Arms and Legs)	42
Arms	42
Legs	43
Proportions	44
Drawing the Human Figure	45
Learning to be Disciplined in Learning Art	49
The Charcoal Summary	51

Visual Communication as an Artist

In these series of "Introduction to Drawing" books, I want to show you how you can improve your drawings by thinking about what you intend to include and dismiss from your artworks. When I look at an artwork, my first thought is: **What is this artwork about**? When creating your own artwork, remember to first establish the main idea or focal point, that is, what the artwork is all about, and what you want to say in creating the artwork. The main idea must remain the focal point in the artwork. Once you have established the main idea or focal point in the artwork, everything you do in the artwork should strengthen that aspect of the artwork.

In art class, the term "values" is used to describe **light and shadows**. "Chiaroscuro" is an Italian artistic term used to describe the dramatic effect of contrasting areas of light and dark in an artwork. Every fully rendered image you draw will be composed of values (darks and lights), regardless of its color. In this book, you will learn how to organize the lights and darks within your charcoal drawing. You will learn how accents and highlights can enhance the objects within your charcoal drawing. Controlling the use of values in an artwork is one way the artist's are able to control the viewer's eyes. An artist uses values as a guide to direct the viewer through the artwork. An artist also uses a hierarchy of values to direct the viewer to what the artist wants the viewer to see first in the artwork. Using values or tones in a charcoal drawing and assigning different areas of a charcoal drawing to lighter or darker tones is commonly done by artists to successfully draw attention to an area in the charcoal drawing quickly, and this has the power to touch viewers of the charcoal drawing emotionally.

As a beginner artist, you are told to observe whatever you are drawing. When you do this, you will discover an unbelievable amount of information through your eyes. You will see an image filled with needless details that will hamper the effectiveness of your artwork. You (the artist) will attempt to reproduce every detail of this image. However, your goal must be to successfully create the artwork by **editing and simplifying** it. When looking at your subject, it helps to squint your eyes to see a simplified version of what you are looking at. Drawing the simple shapes of your subject correctly will help with the overall "soul" of the artwork.

When drawing edges and lines in a charcoal drawing, do not create them with equal thickness. Use both thick and thin lines, because if every line has the same width or is drawn using the same pressure, this will produce a boring and monotoned artwork. In order to make your lines create a livelier artwork, place your lines on the top of the objects, or where the light is directed to be thinner on the objects since the light is hitting the objects at these locations. Add thicker lines underneath the objects since there are usually shadows sitting in these locations.

The benefit of using charcoal is that it is easy to control. You can move it around and remove it or erase it where it is not needed. The eraser can be used as a drawing tool as well, for example, it can be used to create the fur on animals or hair within portraitures.

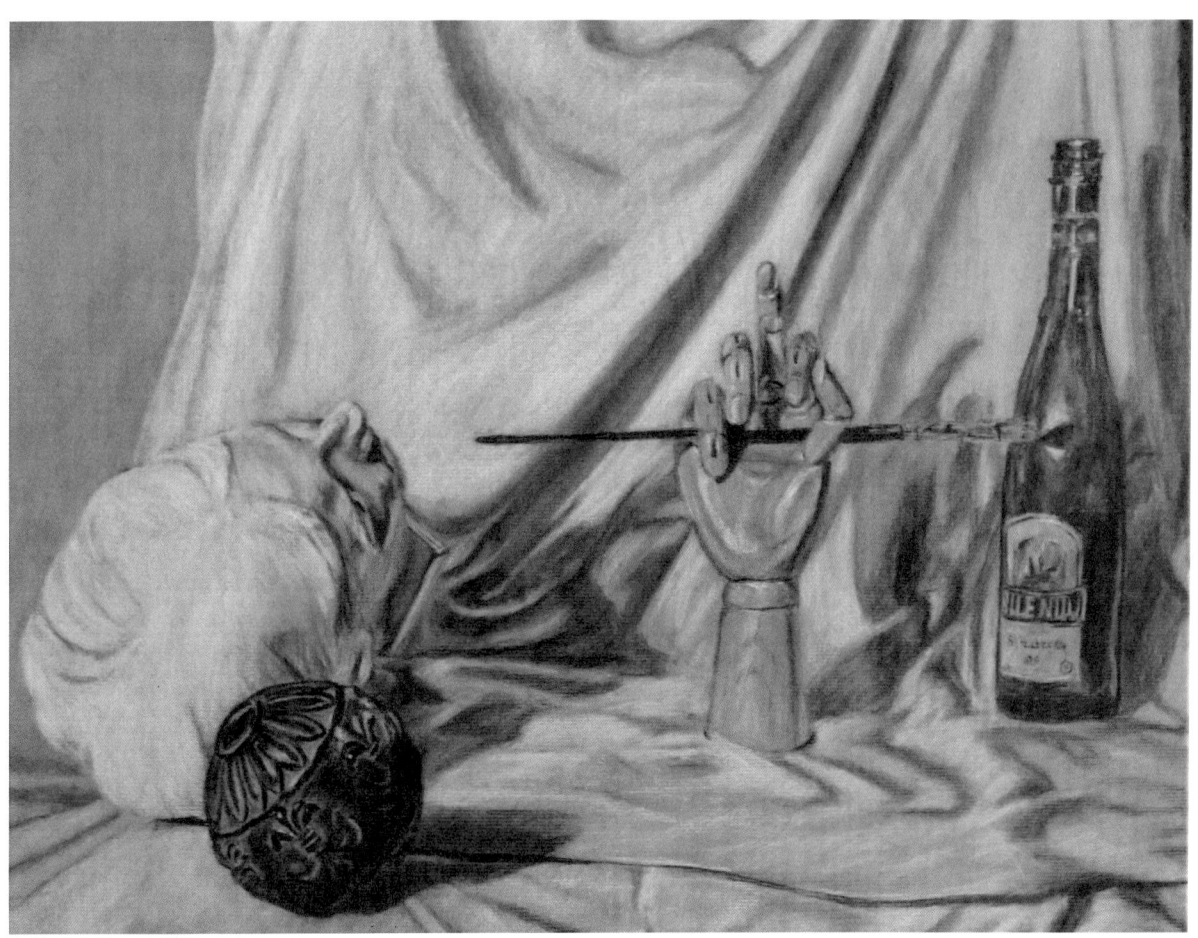

Still Life Charcoal Drawing on Grey Toned Paper

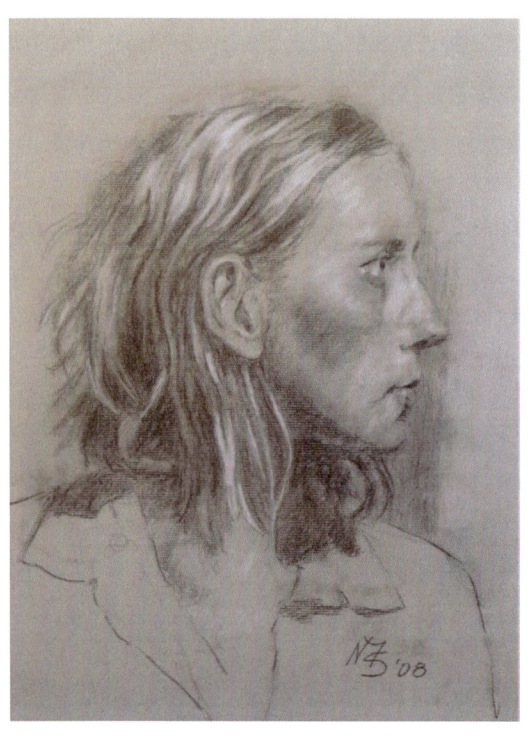 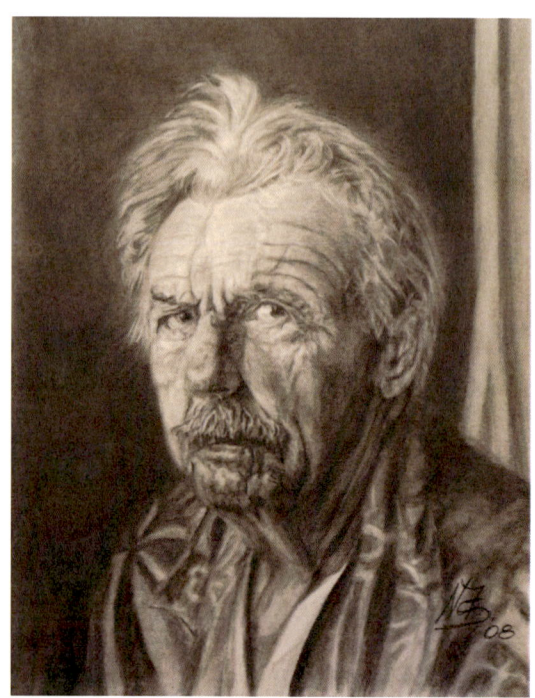

Introduction to Charcoal Drawing

Charcoal has been around for thousands of years and has been identified in ancient cave drawings that most of us have seen. These cave drawings have been found all over the world, from Europe to Australia to Southeast Asia. The soft sticks of black charcoal are the ideal introductory medium for drawing classes. Charcoal comes in various densities, from vine charcoal that produce light strokes to compressed charcoal that create thick dark marks. For a beginner artist, charcoal may be a little difficult to work with, but in time, charcoal will enable you to develop rich tonal values within your artwork as you master this medium. As with all of the drawing mediums, you will have to experiment with them to find out what works for you. The goal here is to learn and discover how to improve your charcoal technique and drawing skills.

I find that most beginners will apply too much pressure when applying charcoal to paper, and doing this will leave marks that are not easily softened or removed. Students should practice developing a sensitive and delicate hand in creating various values, from the blackest black to the lightest grays and in-between tones. This will help students to gain control of the lighter values when applied to their drawings.

I often start my drawings making an initial sketch and outline using vine (also known as willow) charcoal. With vine charcoal you can wipe away mistakes easily. Keep your edge of your outline light and as the drawing evolves slowly, add bolder marks with darker marks when you are confident in their placement.

For most drawing medium, including charcoal, oil is not our friend. Be aware that your hand has oils on them and that can damage the purity of your paper. Oil on your hand can attach to your paper and repel your medium. To solve this problem, wear gloves or place another piece of paper under your hand to protect your artwork.

Like the graphic pencil, charcoal is also not expensive. You can buy willow charcoal, compressed charcoal, charcoal pencils, kneaded eraser, and a sharpener that will create beautiful rich awesome drawings at most any art supply store at a reasonable price.

Charcoal is an ideal medium to learn how to work with tonal values because it does not have color as a distraction. Tonal value is used to create depth, structure, and realism in artworks. Lighter values seem to be protruding, while darker values seem to be pushed inward when using tonal values together.

Charcoal is a natural material, and relatively safe for our health and environment. It is made from branches of the willow tree, or sections of grape vine. One complaint students have is the dust that charcoal produces when drawing. It is important that you do not blow off the dust with your mouth, because you could inhale the charcoal particles. Instead of blowing the charcoal to remove any dust, it would be better to tap your finger on the back of your paper, or use a soft brush or a rag to carefully wipe it away.

Keep in mind that mastering anything, including drawing, is difficult and at times frustrating. Stick to it. Creating art is extremely hard to pull off and it can take time to feel happy about your progress.

Tools and Materials for Drawing with Charcoal

Charcoal drawings will use some of the same materials we used for pencil drawings, but I would like to highlight and add a few items. Artists select materials depending on what they are trying to achieve. You can refer back to Book One for more information on Surfaces and Support, Tracing and Transfer Paper, Eraser and Blending Tool, and Pencil Sharpeners. Remember, this series of "Introduction to Drawing" Books are meant to work together as a collective source of information on drawing.

Try to use the best materials that you can afford, for quality does matter and makes a big difference on the artwork created. Note: Working with new materials takes time to master, so give yourself a little time to experiment as you gain confidence with using new selected materials.

Let's begin with some necessary tools needed to begin our exploration in drawing with charcoal, which are the types of charcoals and various papers used for charcoal drawings.

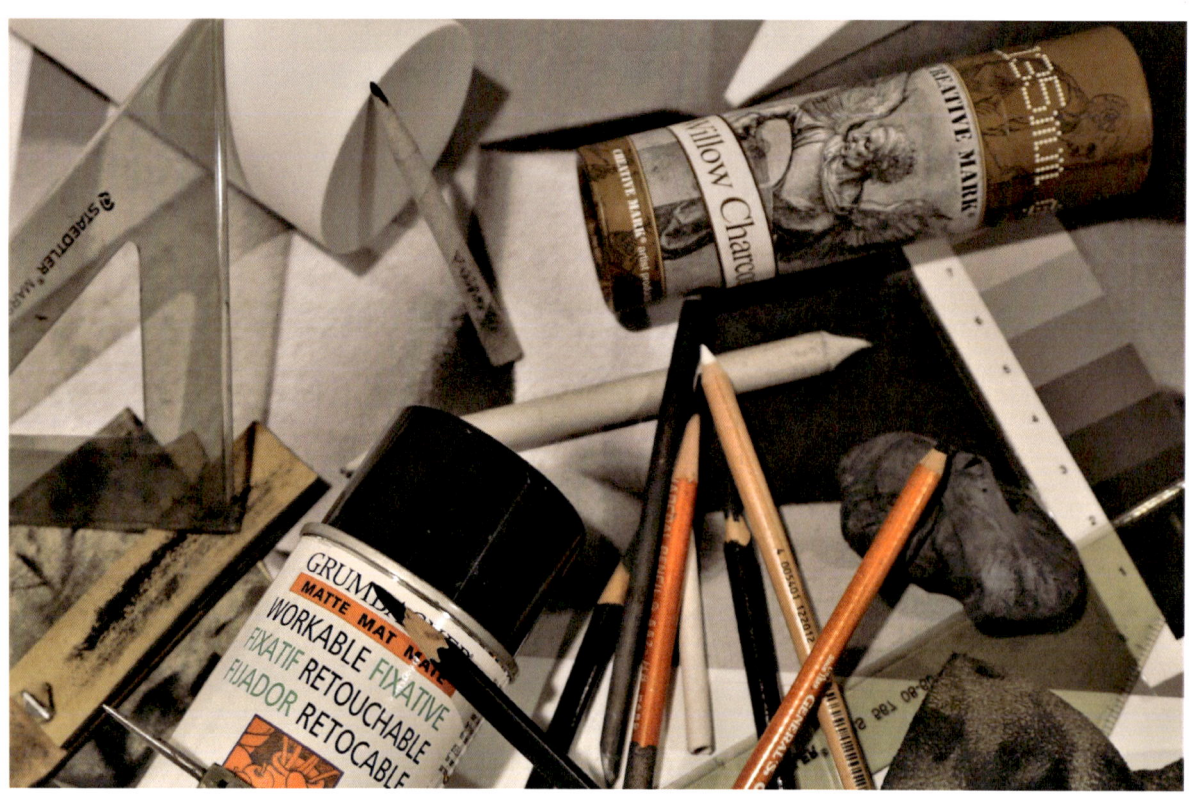

Charcoal Drawing

We covered graphic pencils in Book One of this series, but in this book, I want to highlight the charcoal pencil and associated marking tools. I want to note that there are other types of mediums that are commonly used in combination with the charcoal pencil. Two commonly used mediums are the compressed charcoal, which can produce a rich dark black tone, and the vine or willow charcoal, which is lighter in tone and easier to erase than the compressed charcoal and the white pastel or white conté crayons pencil. Conté crayons or conté sticks are a drawing medium composed of compressed powdered graphite or charcoal mixed with a wax or clay base. Conté crayons or Conté sticks come in various colors and act like charcoal, with the exception that they are much stronger and difficult to remove. If you are working on toned paper (usually gray or tan), you can use black charcoal or brown pastel pencils to create the shadows, toned paper to create the middle tones, and white conté or white pastel pencil to create the highlights on your drawing.

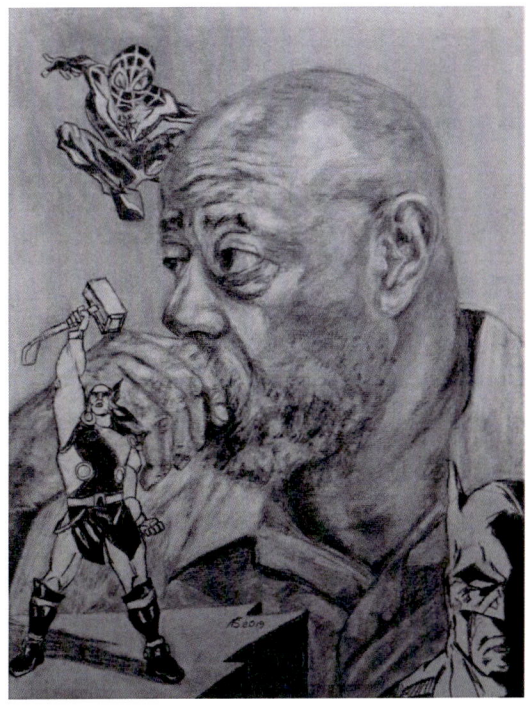

**Charcoal on Charcoal Paper,
Story Teller, 18" X 24"**

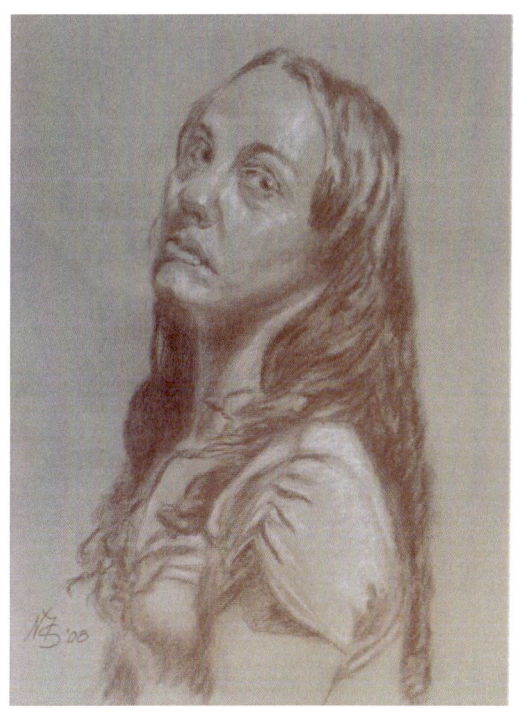

**Pastel on Tan Color Paper,
Portrait Study, 18" X 24"**

Marking Tools for Charcoal Drawings

Charcoal Pencils

Like the Graphite pencil, the charcoal pencil is a tool that should feel very comfortable to most of us. Just like the graphite pencil, the charcoal pencil has a wide range of tones (values). When working with any art tool, including the charcoal pencil, select the best quality that you can afford. The charcoal pencil is composed of compressed charcoal surrounded by a protective covering, commonly wood. The charcoal pencil is ideal for sketching and drawing and provides the artist with control over their marks. Charcoal is a medium that can create rick and dark tones, as well as thin and bold lines. You are looking for a quality pencil that creates smooth and uniform lines.

Some makers of good quality pencils are **General**, who manufactured charcoal pencils that are smooth and uniform. The pencils have little drag, take to bleeding and are reasonably priced. **Derwent's** charcoal pencils are not as soft as **General** charcoal pencils, making them a little scratchier, but they produce cleaner lines and do not smudge as easily. For the experienced charcoal user, the **Koh-I-Noor Gioconda** charcoal pencil set is a perfect choice. The charcoal produces rich tone with a satin-like finish. It is great for creating beautiful tonal studies. The **Koh-I-Noor Gioconda** Charcoal Pencil also comes in sepia dark and sepia light.

In starting out, I suggest you use HB, 2B and 6B pencils, as well as a 5B white charcoal pencil to create highlights. Try not to drop your charcoal pencils, because they may shatter internally, making it impossible to resharpen. Speaking of sharpening, the charcoal pencils can snap in a regular hand sharpener, so it may be wise to invest in a compatible sharpener to maintain a pointy tip or the use of a X-Acto knife. It is important to have a correct point on your pencil, which can be achieved by rubbing the charcoal along a sandpaper block.

Willow or Vine Charcoal Sticks

With willow or vine charcoal sticks, you will be able to create broader strokes by laying the sticks flat on their sides or use them to make a variety of lines using the ends of the sticks. I use vine charcoal to create gray-toned backgrounds using the side of the stick to cover large areas of the drawing surface. I also use the willow or vine charcoal to draw my initial lines for drawing, for I find the willow or vine charcoal easy to remove. Once I can see the drawing clearly, I go over the willow or vine charcoal with a charcoal pencil, which is a little less ease to remove.

Other Forms of Charcoal

Charcoal comes in a variety of forms, such as the pencil and vine (willow) already discussed. It also comes as compressed sticks or powder. You can use rags, paper towel, or stump to create a soft look. You can create a number of textures by using a paint brush, rag, or eraser. Your selections of papers will change the outcome of the medium. Many different applications and effects can be created and a number of different looks can be achieved from soft and smooth to expressive and raw.

Paper for Charcoal Drawing

In order for artists to select the best paper for any medium, they must keep in mind the characteristics of the medium and what desired outcome they would like to create. In using medium such as charcoal or pastel, the surface that is best suited is one that has a fair amount of texture. Also, in selecting paper, you should select a surface that is durable, and has a surface that is not so delicate that it will not stand up to being roughened by marking, blending, or erasing. When using black and white charcoal, make sure not to mix the black and white marks creating a gray on gray tones on the drawing.

Newsprint

Newsprint is commonly used when we are being introduced to charcoal drawing because it is affordable. At the beginning stages of drawing, you are only practicing and getting familiar with the medium. The drawback of newsprint is that it is fairly thin, so it can tear and buckle under strong pressure. Newsprint is a smooth paper and great for graphite, but it doesn't hold charcoal or pastel, as well as drawing paper, with a rougher texture. The surface texture is described as the paper's "tooth" or how the surface holds the medium. The softer your medium, the more tooth you want. So, in general, the soft toothed paper would not be a great selection for charcoal paper. Common charcoal or pastel paper have a texture you will want. The paper is 60-90-lb. Some common papers would be Canson Mi-Teintes, Canson-Ingres, Strathmore 500 Series, and Fabriano Tiziano.

Toned Paper

The color of toned paper can greatly enhance a drawing, if you select the right temperature and value that is suited for your art subject. Gray papers with a mixture of black and white charcoal give a lot of visual impact.

Fixative (Workable)

Artists working with charcoal and pastel drawings will sometimes need to spray their work with fixative to lock the medium in place. Make sure that you use workable fixative, for this allows you to continue to make changes and corrections to your artwork after it has been sprayed. Before using the fixative, experiment with the fixative, especially the spray angle and distance from the artwork surface, to ensure you get the results you desire. Various fixatives will affect the color and surface texture of your drawing, so experiment on scrap paper first. Also use the fixative outside or in a well vented area.

Final Notes on Paper

When creating finished artworks, as opposed to practice drawing or sketches, use acid-free (pH level of seven). Be aware of the oil on your fingers and hands so as not to smudge the artwork. Use a higher "PLY" paper. The higher the ply number, the thicker the paper. The thicker paper will stand up to the kind of pressure produced with charcoal. Select a paper that has a good texture.

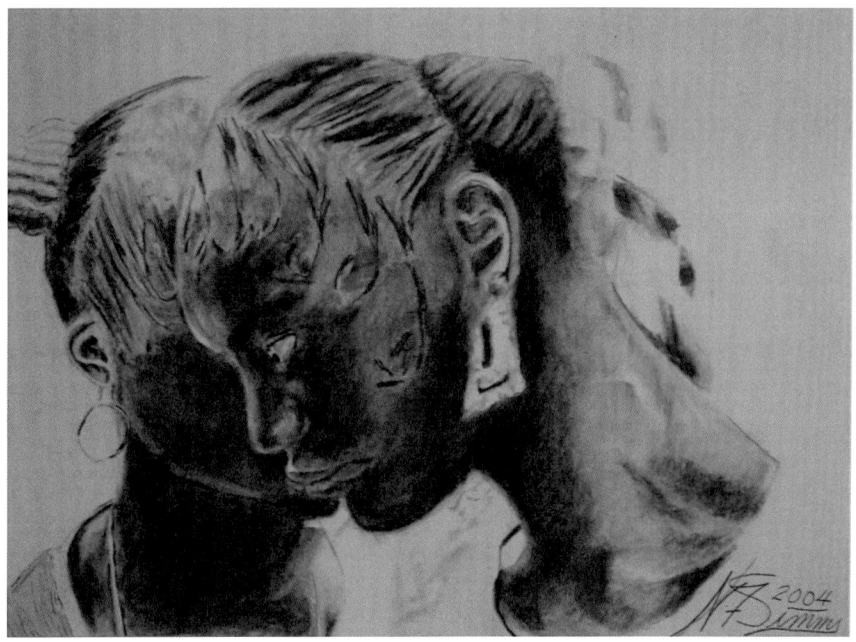

Secrets, 14" X 20", Charcoal on Charcoal Paper

Shading

Drawing the outline of an object is the foundation of creating a believable and compatible object. Knowing how to apply tones of various light and dark areas and how to apply shading will increase the likelihood of the object appearing real. This is because shading can show the effects of curving and the illusion of forms of objects. In shading objects, artists have to understand where the lights and shadows are located on the objects and what values to apply to the areas of objects in order to create an illusion of realism. The difference in values tones is called contrast. How light or dark these values tones are depends on the value and light within your drawing. Before we begin, let's get a better understanding of values used in creating realistic art forms.

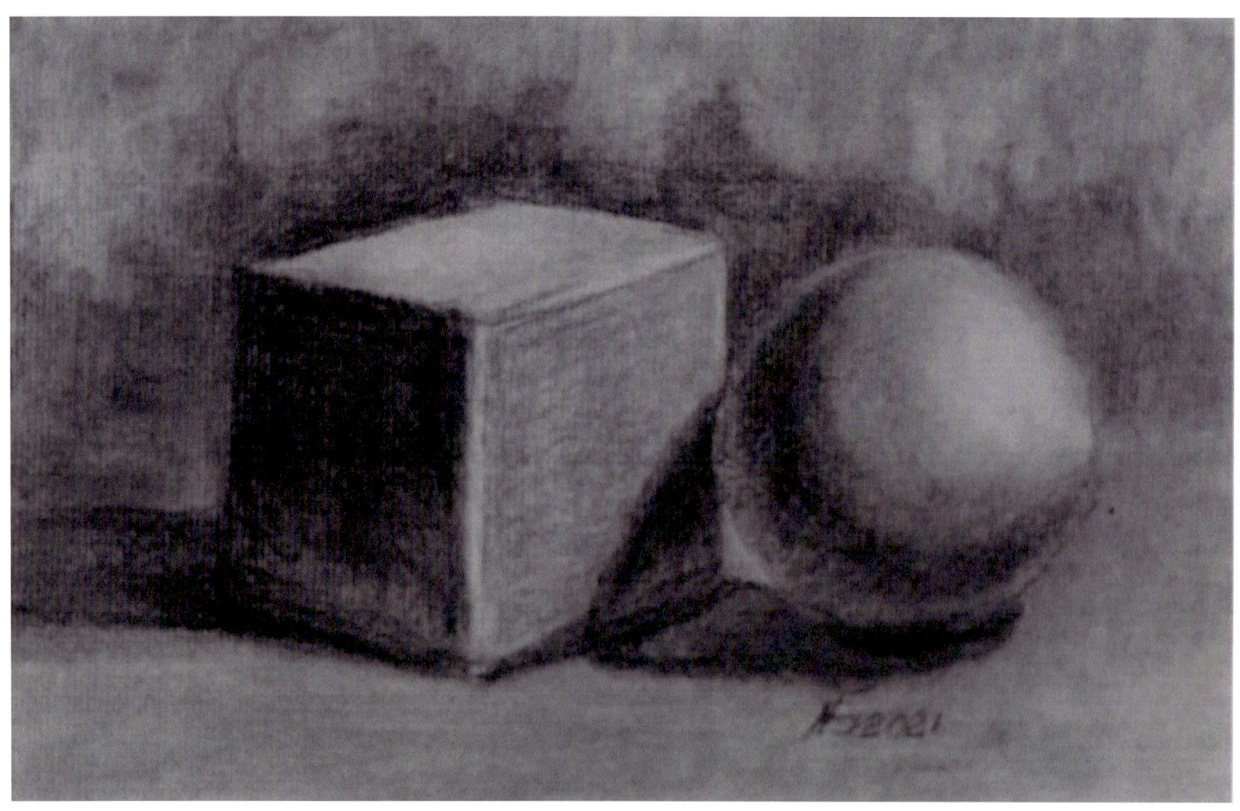

Geometric Shapes, Charcoal on Drawing Paper

Light and Dark Values

What are values referring to in art? Value is the lightness to darkness range of a color or tone that we see on objects when light is hidden from or projected onto it. Light reflects off objects into our eyes and our minds interpret that light and rationalize what we see. Values are the key to the illusion of form in realistic artworks. Chiaroscuro is what you may refer to as shading. The American pronunciation is (Kee-aa-ruh-skyur-ow). It is an Italian word describing the effect of contrasting areas of light and dark in an artwork. The ancient Greek and Roman artists used chiaroscuro effects, but Leonardo da Vinci in the late 15th century brought it to its full potential.

In working with shading and values, we will give the light and shadows names and associate them with numbers from one to seven. One is the lightest and seven is the darkest, as shown in the illustration below.

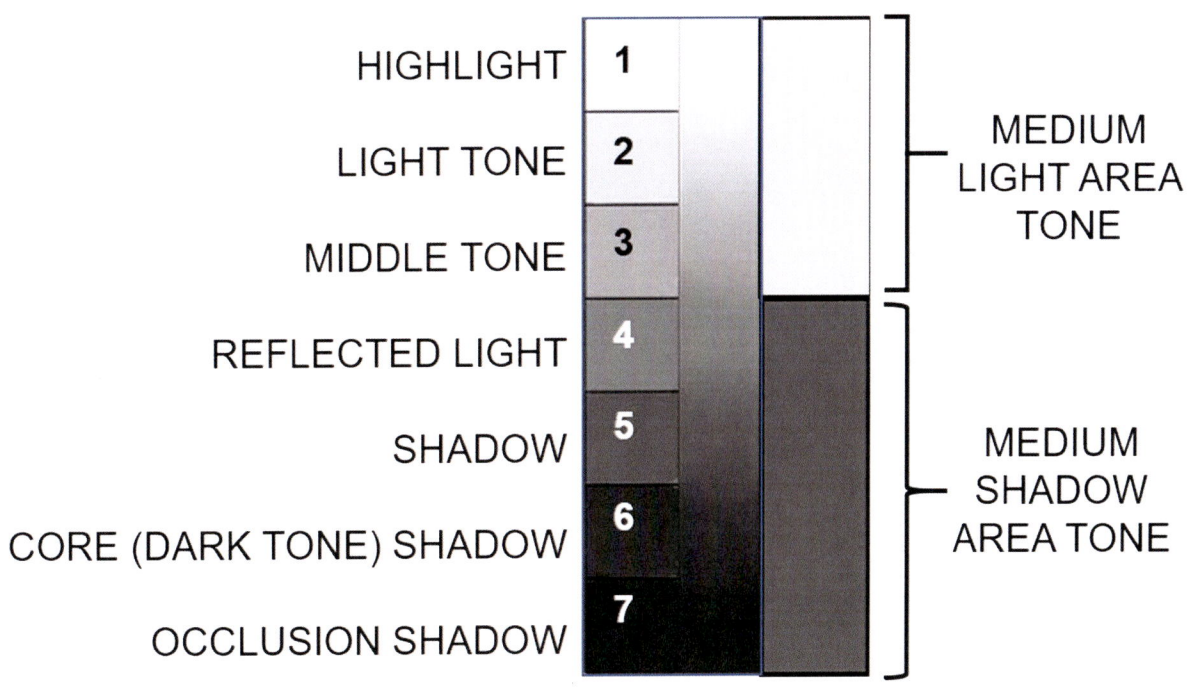

Chiaroscuro Values for Solid Forms

You will commonly see the Values on charts numbered, indicating the degrees of darkness to lightness. To realistically create an illusion of any subject, we must understand how to render both cast shadows (consisting of hard-edges) and form shadows. We can break the various values into categories:

1. Highlight: the lightest areas.

2. Light: the area between and around the highlight approaching the halftone planes in the light.

3. Form shadow: The portion of the form that is in shadow, lying in a plane where light cannot reach, creating a (consisting of soft-edges) gradual transition from light to shadow.

4. Cast shadow: The trailing edge of the form shadow. All shadows begin as soft-edged form shadows and end as hard-edged cast shadows.

5. Reflected light: Found only in form shadows, where light is reflected back onto the surface of the shadow area.

Applying Light and Shadows

We will be partially reviewing what we have learned, and in addition, learning a little about shading facial proportions.

In creating believable realistic three-dimensional drawings on a flat surface, I will show you how to apply value tones on solid objects, facial figures, and later in this book, body figures within your drawings. Shading and proportion are the two essential key elements that will accomplish realism within any artwork. Before we start, I will show you some typical measurements on how the adult human face is organized.

First, let's get familiar with some terms used for Shading artwork by looking at the values applied to the sphere below.

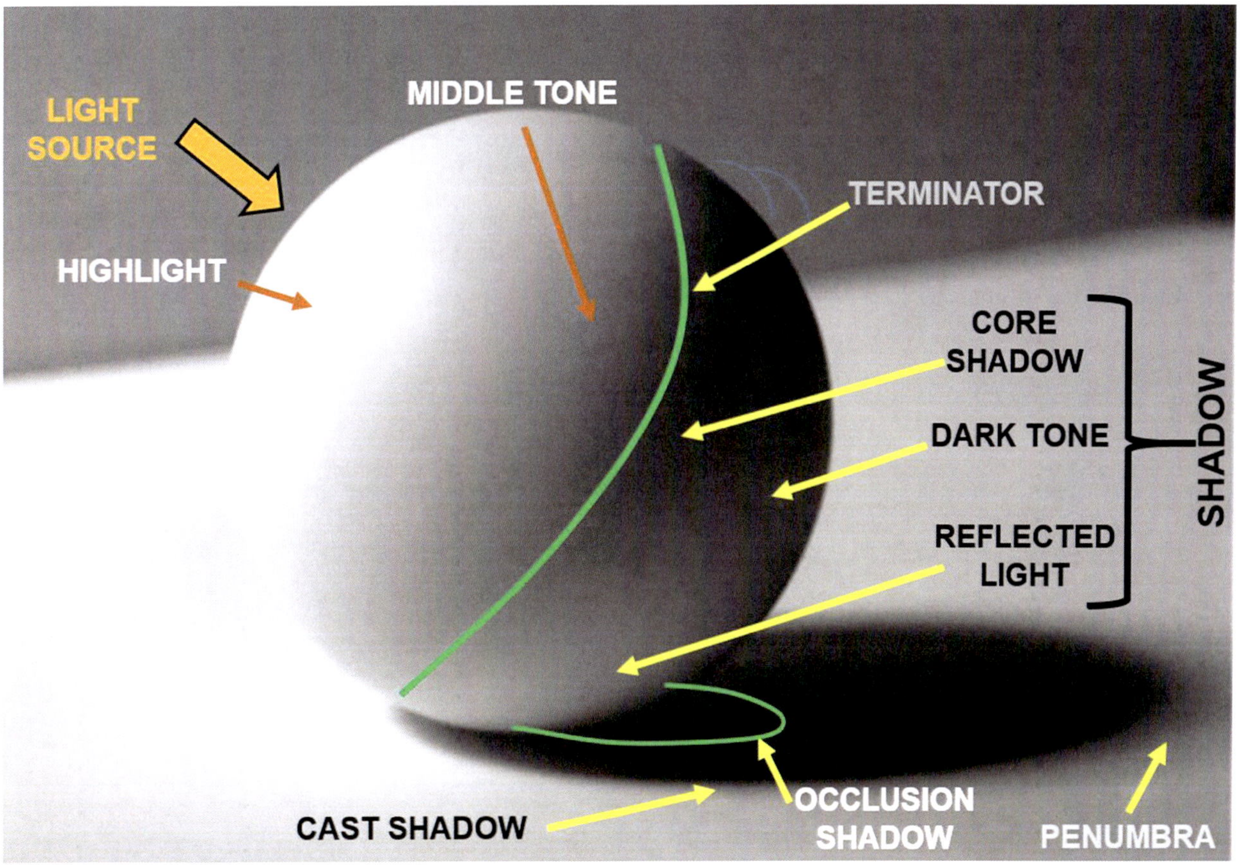

Assignment: BK 2-01 Shading on White Charcoal Paper

Draw and Shade the Object on this page using Charcoal on White Charcoal paper.

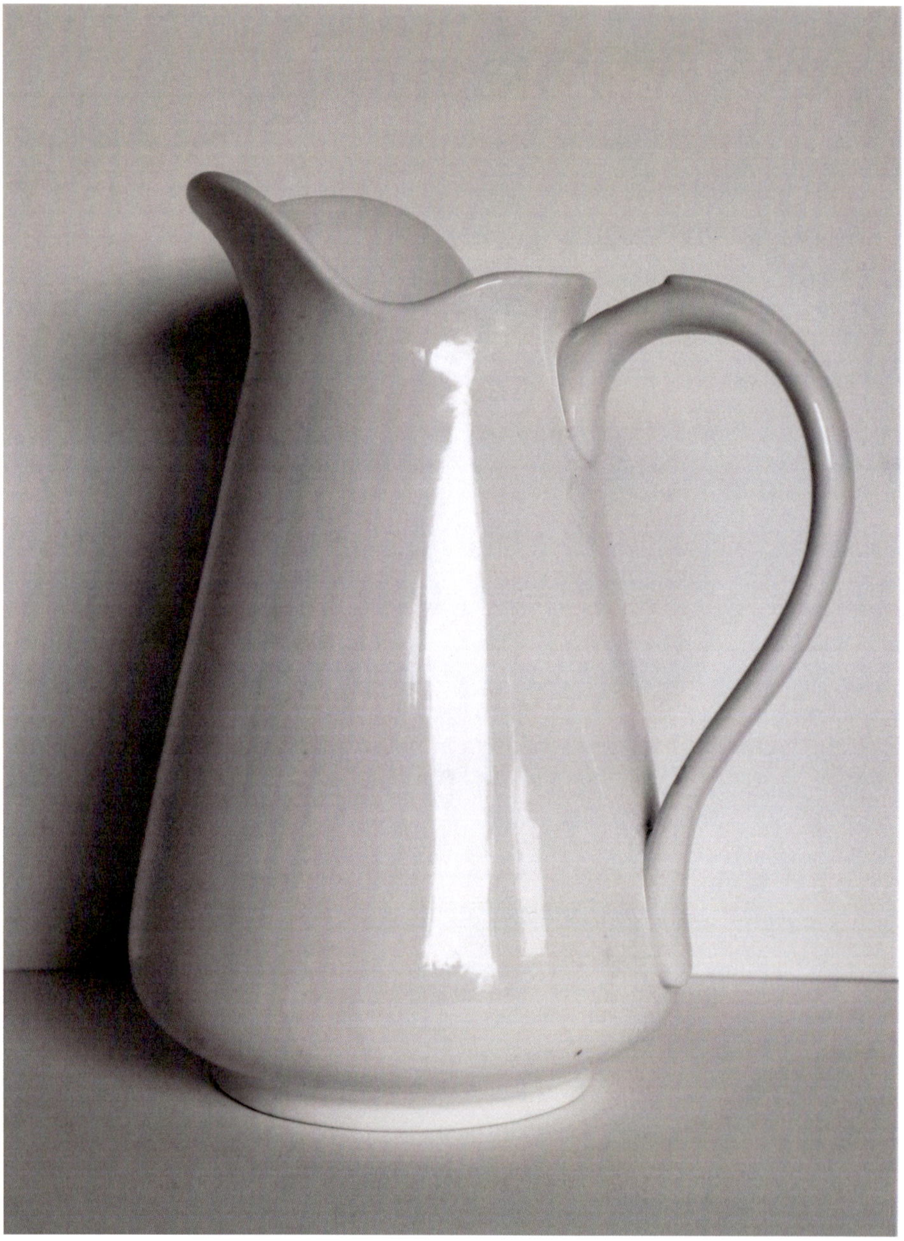

Assignment: BK 2-02 Shading on Gray Toned Paper

Draw and Shade the Group of Objects on this page using Charcoal on Gray toned paper.

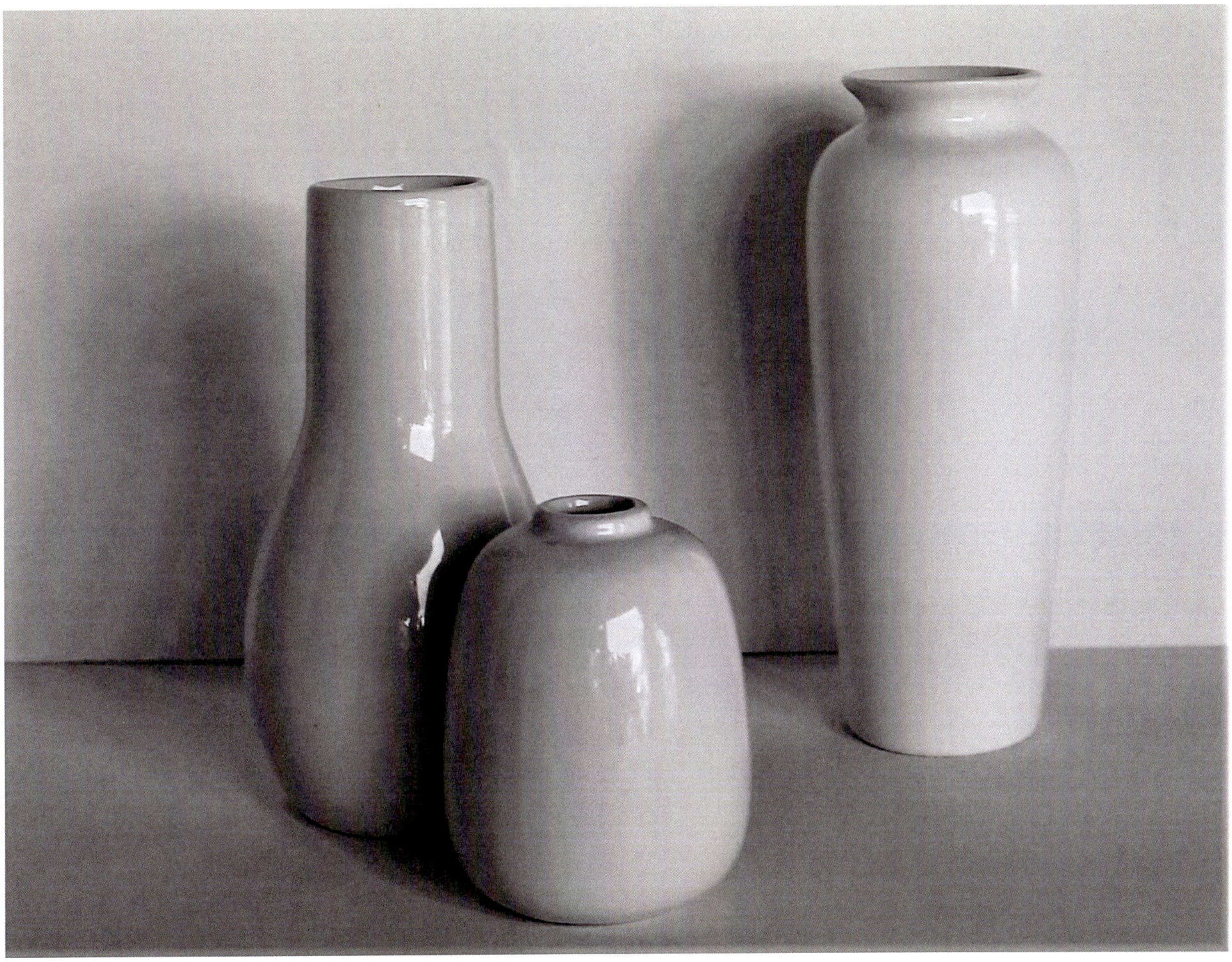

Quiz BK 2-01 (Shading)

1.1 What role does shading have in creating realistic drawing?

1.2 Why are values important to artists?

1.3 What is the difference between form shadows and cast shadows?

1.4 What is meant by soft and hard edges in art?

1.5. How important is the understanding of light and shadows in realistic artworks?

Quiz BK 2-01 Answers

1.1 Shading with the understanding of values and their placements (indicating highlights and shadows) will create realism.

1.2 Values create contrast, which is needed for the viewer to see and be drawn to the areas of the highest contrast. This is only one of the ways that artists use to show the viewer what they are indicating what is important.

1.3 Form shadow is created by light on a subject which on the opposite side will create a shadow, whereas Cast shadow is created by light being blocked by some object that restricts the light from passing thereby creating a shadow.

1.4 Soft edges are mostly seen on form shadows where the change in values are gradual. Hard edges are seen where the values change edges are razor shape.

1.5. In creating convincing realistic drawings, add value to create the illusion of form, by using lights and shadows. The drawing will appear three-dimensional and the rendering will communicate volume because of the application of shading.

Facial Features Locations

Now, let's get an understanding of where things generally are located on the adult human face, so that we can create a template. This will aid us with placement of our proportions of facial features, so that they are fairly correct. We are going to simplify the diagram below by using simple shapes to guide our measurements.

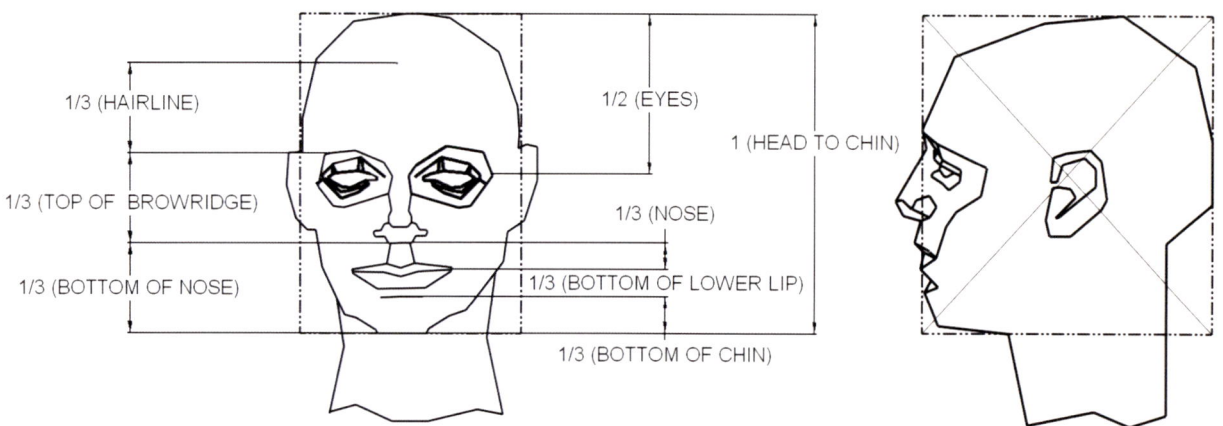

Work with the Still-Life drawings to practice using charcoal as a medium that is excellent in applying values. When drawing human faces and bodies, form and proportion are important in creating realistic drawings. However, the artist does not always start drawing the features first. By creating and placing the light and shadows first, this will create a likeness before any features (eyes, nose, lips) are added.

We will slowly approach drawing the female plaster casted face on the next page, one step at a time. We will learn to create a template that will establish a guide for placing the features in the correct locations.

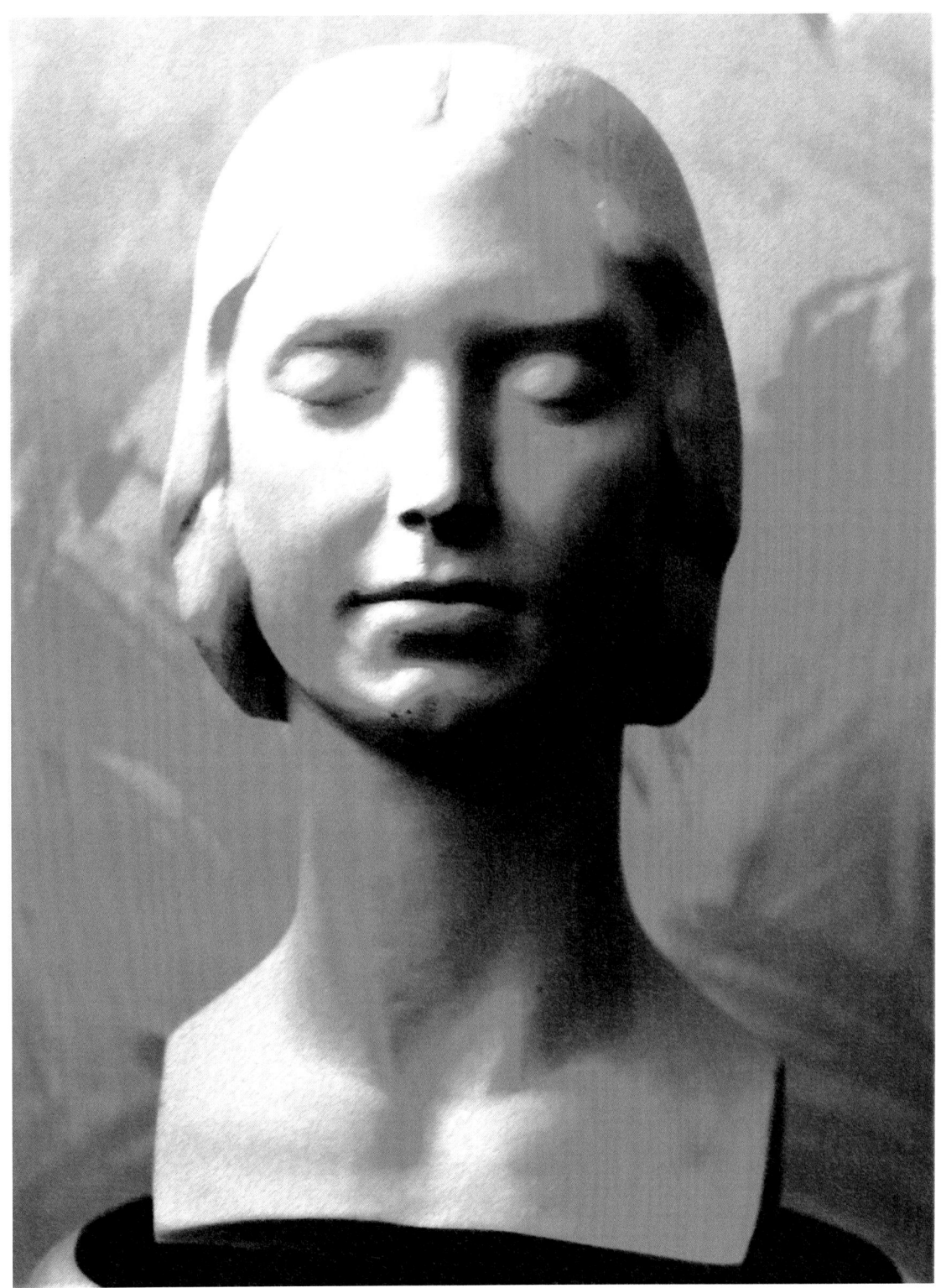

Reference Female Frontal Face Features

Steps in Creating a Facial Template

STEP ONE

Create a face template by drawing a circle, and in the middle of the circle, draw a square as shown below in red.

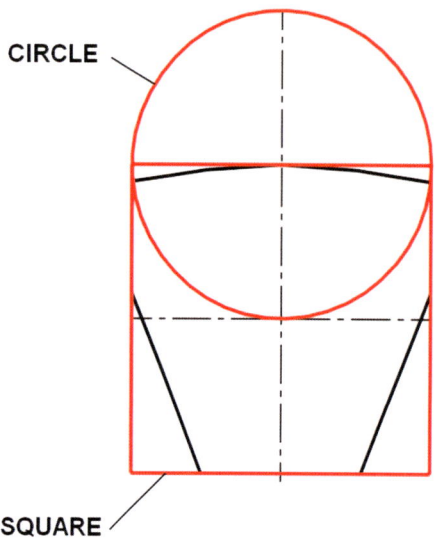

STEP TWO

Modify the square as shown below in red. Note that we have created a proportional map of the face, locating the top of the head, the top of the brow ridge, the bottom of the nose, and the bottom of the chin.

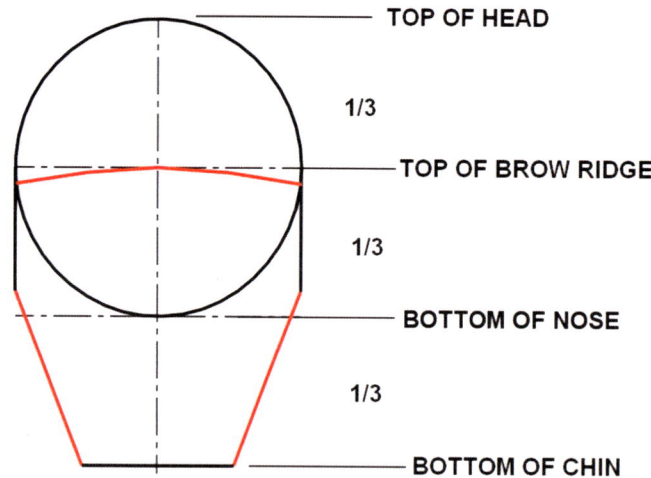

STEP THREE

Draw a line from the outer corners of the eyes. Draw a line from the ends of that line to the middle and to the bottom of the lip's location, creating a triangle. Locate the middle of the eyes and the outer ends of the mouth, and draw a vertical line between them as shown below in red.

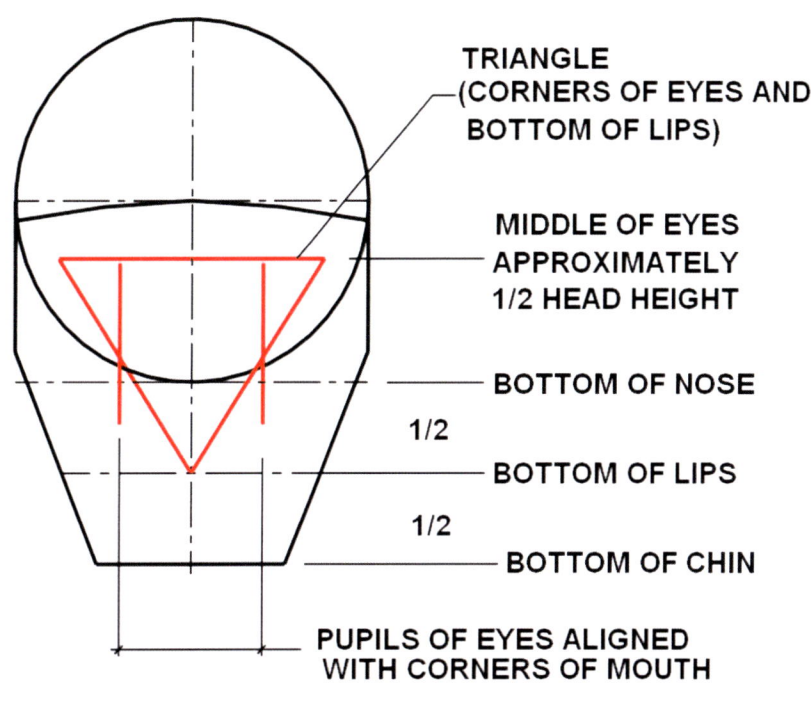

FACIAL FEATURES RELATIONSHIPS

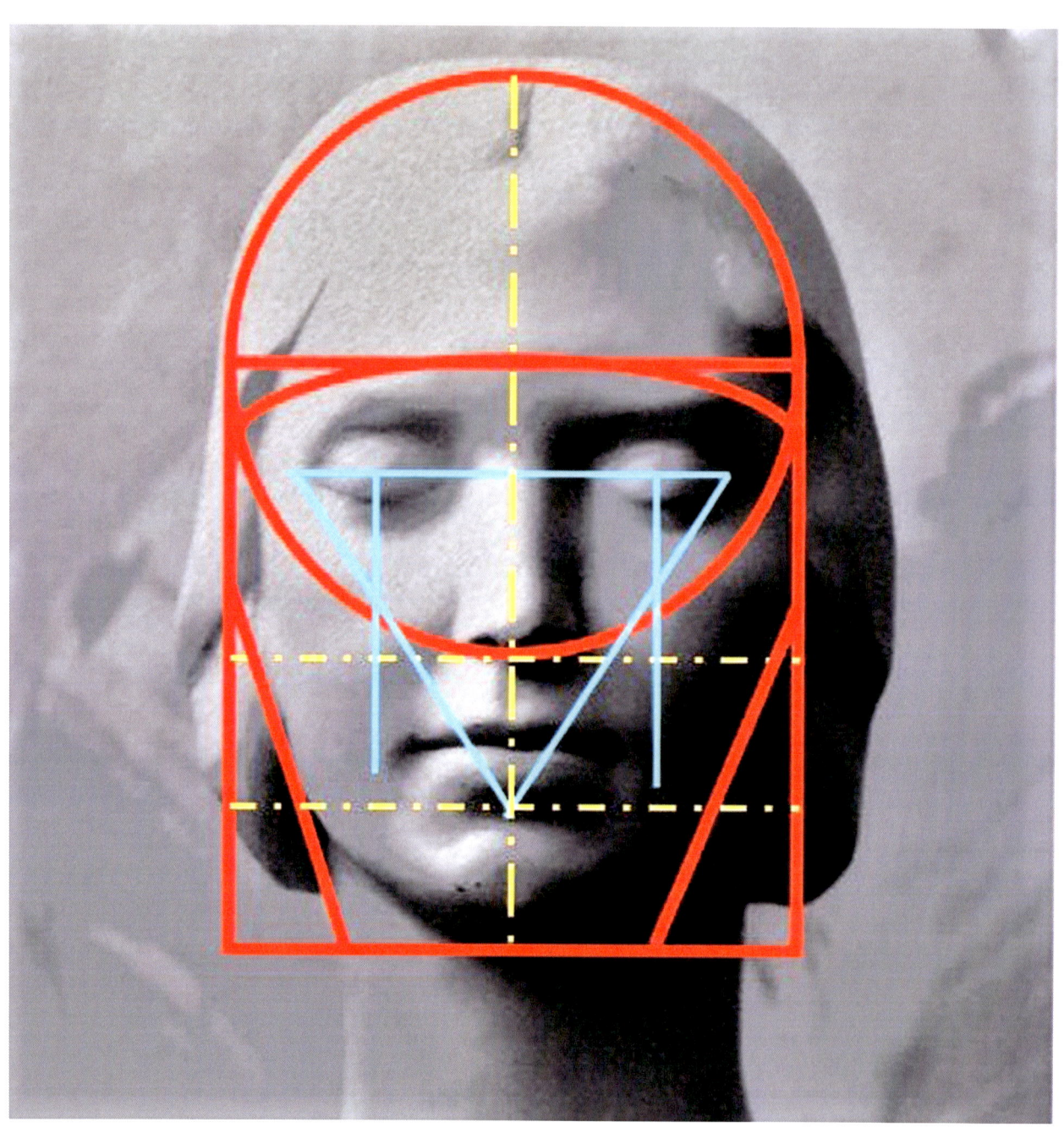

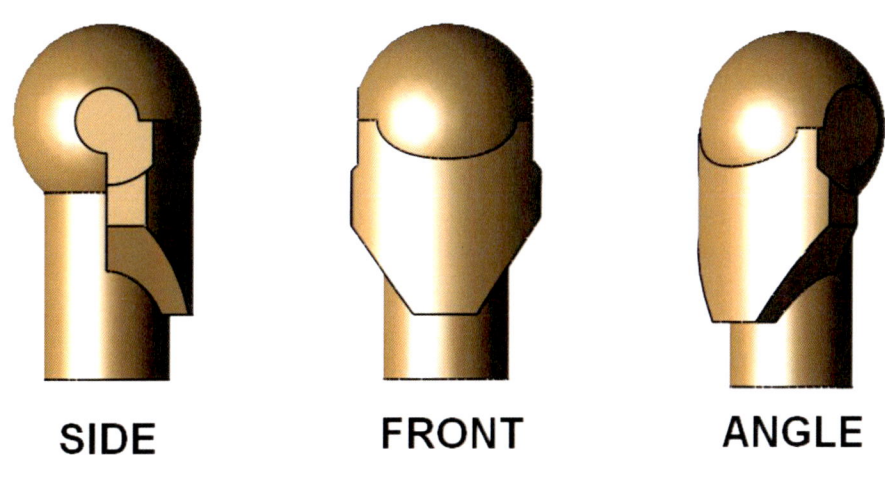

SIDE　　FRONT　　ANGLE

3-DIMENSIONAL HEAD TEMPLATES

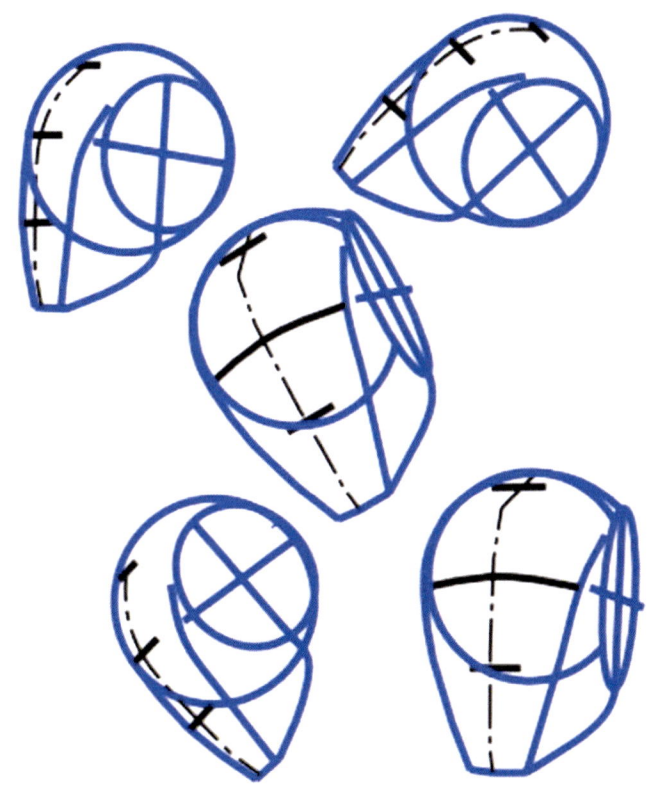

USE YOUR TEMPLATE TO DRAW THE HEAD AT VARIOUS ANGLES AND DIRECTIONS

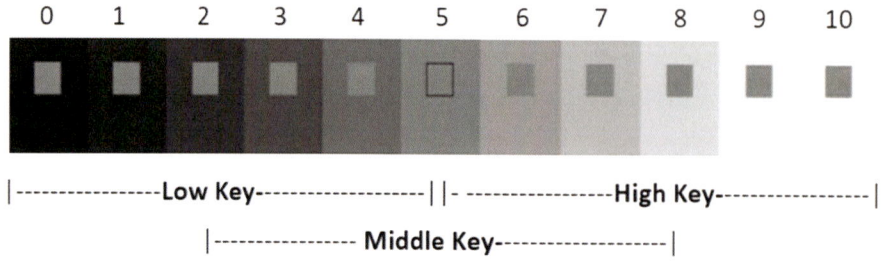

Gray Scale and Key Value Ranges

Value Keys

Artworks generally fall into three categories of Keys or Moods. Value Keys play an important role in creating mood and aiding in the artwork concept that you are trying to display. There are other elements of art that will create mood, but for now, we will focus on the role Values play.

The three Key Value Ranges are:

1) High Key: A high key artwork is one that is predominantly light in values. If colors are used, they are pastels, and the mood is often light hearted, friendly or romantic. Artworks (*i.e.*, drawings and paintings) are light and airy.

2) Low Key: A low key artwork uses predominantly dark values. If your desire is to convey an ominous, serious or mysterious mood, then this is the key you want to consider using.

3) Mid or Intermediate Key: Most artworks end up in the mid or intermediate key where middle values dominate the artworks. It is important to note that intermediate key artworks often do not contain as much drama or emotion as low or high key artworks — not always, but often.

Lines and Values create Shape or Volume Masses. We will look at Values for Drawing Outdoors or Atmosphere (Landscape) and Values used for Form (Still-Life, Figures).

Working with Landscape Artworks

Landscape art depicts nature (mountains, valleys, trees, rivers, and so on). In order to create a 3-dimensional illusion on a 2-dimensional surface, the artist uses several methods to indicate space. Objects placed in front, overlapping another object, will appear closer, and objects placed behind will appear further in the background. Objects that are closest to us will appear larger in size, and will become smaller visually in size as they recede farther away. Objects located at the bottom of the picture will advance forward, and objects placed toward the top of the picture will visually move back in space. There is more contrast value and details and sharpness as objects get closer, and less contrast and sharpness as objects move farther visually from us.

Good landscape artworks should all define a predefined outline of spaces, that should clearly delineate the foreground, middle ground and background subjects. The artist should clearly show and place attention on the focal point within the artwork. Use cropping effectively to aid the viewer to understand and focus on the focal areas (points of interest). Simplify the composition structure's arrangement.

Composition in landscape art is how the artist decides to arrange the placement of elements to create the artwork. In creating the composition, the artist is determining how to create a focal point, mood, and directional cues that will help the viewer navigate through the artwork. Composition is a very important feature of any artwork, but for landscapes, it is surprisingly often overlooked by amateur artists. One reason that artists will create poor compositional artworks is because they rarely spend time in planning to create a work of art. They simply copy what they see or from some photographs, exactly as they see it. This often creates a bad composition.

Working with Landscape Artworks - Step by Step

Step 1: *First, sketch the larger general shapes of the scene – this means no details, just basic shapes.*

The first thing you must learn is the KISS principle (Keep It Simple Stupid). Find a landscape that needs little if any changes - one that will create a successful composition. Divide the landscape in flat silhouettes of foreground, middle ground, and background of light and dark values. Apply the middle tone values in the large basic shapes (circle, square or rectangle, triangle, polygon) – not the object. By doing this, you will see if your overall design is working early on.

Note: If you are preparing to work outdoors, you will need a folding chair, umbrella, paper towels, and sunglasses. You may also need a portable small easel and a camera for reference. Go outdoors or look out of your window to sketch. There is nothing that can compare to working with the real thing. A lot of information is lost in photographs. Use the camera for reference only when creating landscapes. When working outside, do not draw more than three hours at a time. In the outdoors, the shadows' shapes dramatically change. This is also a reason not to use a surface larger than 11" X 14". Larger artworks

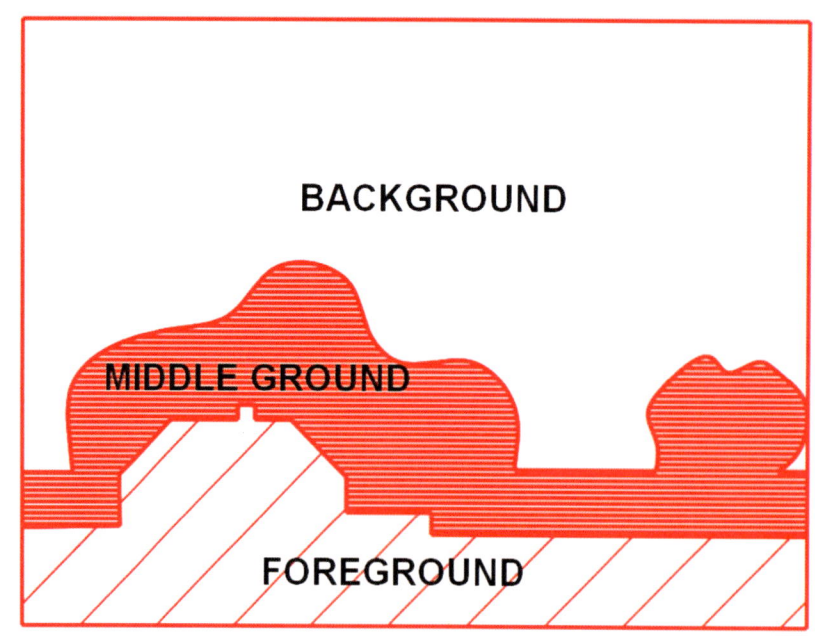

can be done in the studio.

Step 2: *Second, emphasize the main subject, i.e., the center of interest, by using stronger value contrasts on or close around your subject.*

Your landscape art should always have a definite subject. There is only one hard rule for the placement of your main subject, and that rule is: Do not put the subject dead center or in the middle (horizontally or vertically) of the picture. Always emphasize the subject by using contrast (strong differences) on and near it.

Nature is overwhelming which makes it difficult for the beginning artist to select scenes because of complexity. Here are five suggestions for selecting your subjects:

1. Do not expect to find the perfect picture. As an artist, you have to be selective by moving or leaving out objects that conflict with the main subject.

2. Limit yourself to only a few simply subjects. Remember you have to manage the relationships of size, shape, color, and details for the art to work.

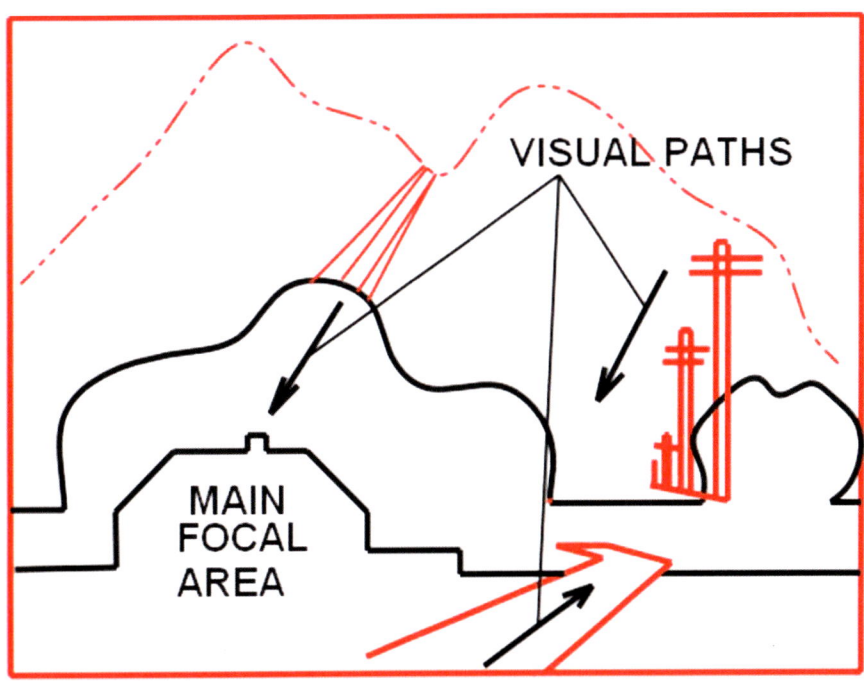

28

3. You are an artist, not a tourist. Anything and everything around you can become a great work of art. Pick a subject, for example, rocks, a building, a group of boats docked at a lake. Everything around you is a worthwhile subject to explore.

4. Do not be afraid to add man-made objects, figures or animals to your artwork.

5. Eliminate or simplify details to unify the effects in a larger artwork.

Step 3. *Third, balance your landscape and provide a visual path. Add tone, texture, and color, if applicable, in order to enhance a feeling of solidness and unity to the sketch, drawing or painting.*

Artists do not copy nature precisely. After determining and placing your subject off-center; the artist must move things and add and subtract elements to balance the picture. A typical fault of many student artists is the lack of contrast. On the other extreme, many student artists lavish too much detail on each object. The artist is the director of his picture and should lead the viewer's eyes along a path to the center of interest. The visual path may be lines, hills, roads or even stepping stones. Adding a visual path such as a row of fence posts will improve your work tremendously.

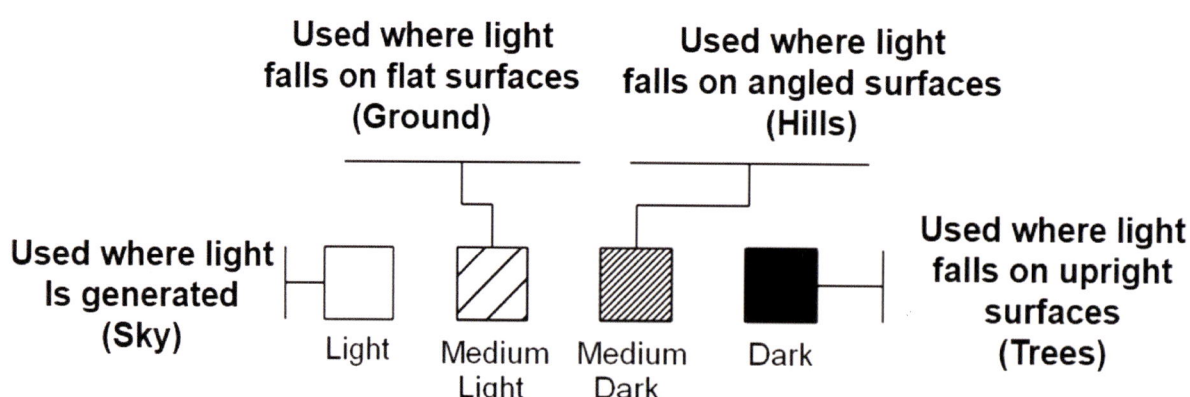

Four Values used in Landscapes

Step 4. *Fourth, finish the artwork by showing the elements of perspective, refining it by carefully adding details. Remember the goal is to focus details and emphasize the main focal subject.*

We are able to show space and depth in landscapes by using the principles of overlap, position, size, detail, value and color. The values in the foreground will be strong and dark, with strong contrast and detail, while those values farther away will usually seem lighter, with less contrast and details. Artists refer to these changes in detail, value, and color as atmospheric aerial perspective.

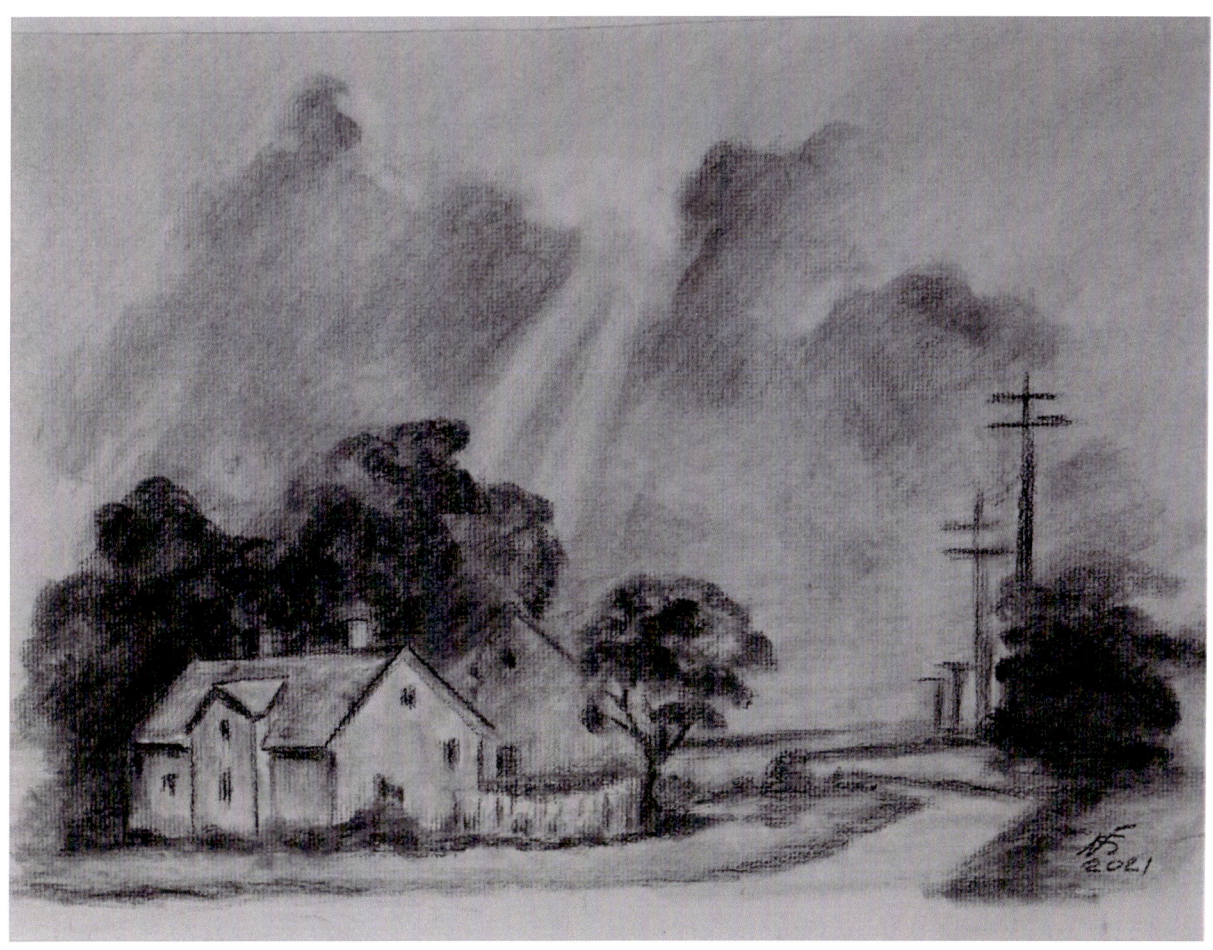

Landscape Study, 12" X 16, Charcoal on Charcoal Paper

Quiz BK 2-02 (Applying Values to Landscapes)

1.1. In creating a landscapes, the Steps that should typically be used in order are:
   A. Add Shading
   B. Add Definition and Refine detail
   C. Draw Simple Basic Shapes
   D. Compose a Center of Interest (Focal Point)

1.2. What is the most important part of creating a landscape artwork?
   A. Focal Points
   B. Transitions
   C. Unity and Balance
   D Lines and Paths
   E. All (A,B,C and D)

1.3 As subjects recede into the landscape, they will most often become:
   A. Larger
   B. Lighter and Smaller
   C. Farther Apart
   D. More Detailed

1.4 What is Landscape artwork?

Quiz BK 2-02 Answers

1.1. In creating a landscapes, the Steps that should typically be used in order are:

   C, A, D, and B.

1.2. What is the most important part of creating a landscape artwork?

   E. All (A,B,C and D)

1.3 As subjects recede into the landscape, they will most often become:

   B. Lighter and Smaller

1.4 What is Landscape artwork?

Landscape art typically includes natures scenery. We would include mountains, forests, cliffs, trees, rivers, valley. It is not uncommon that man made objects, such as barns, houses. boats, fences, etc., would make their way into landscape art. Also, people (man, woman, and children) and animals (horses, cows, or birds) are often included in landscape artworks.

The Art of Nudes

In both the works of past artists [such as the French artist Pierre-Paul Prud'hon (1758-1823) or the Italian artist Michelangelo di Lodovico Buronarrorti Simoni (1475-1564)], and the present master artists of the twenty-first century [such as Anthony (Tony) Ryder or Costa Vavagiakis and many others], the nude figure is still very much admired. However, we are at an age where many do not think about the importance of the nude figure or consider it appropriate as fine art to be hung in their homes. The reasons for this are due to people's inability to see beyond the implied negative sexuality of the nude figure, and to separate the representation of the ideal arrangements of beautiful forms from the massive pornography and sexual images that are distributed on the internet and in publications and advertisements.

Still, drawing and painting the nude figure is one of the best ways to increase your creativity and drawing ability. This is because the human body, although it has its proportions, is also alive, and to recreate this life, the artist cannot reproduce the human life form's gesture and spirit in the same manner as he or she would create a still life artwork. The nude figure is foremost a beautiful work of art within itself. It is a challenge for the artist to create a divine work of art, full of energy, passion, and a host of other wonderful moods, within a drawing or painting.

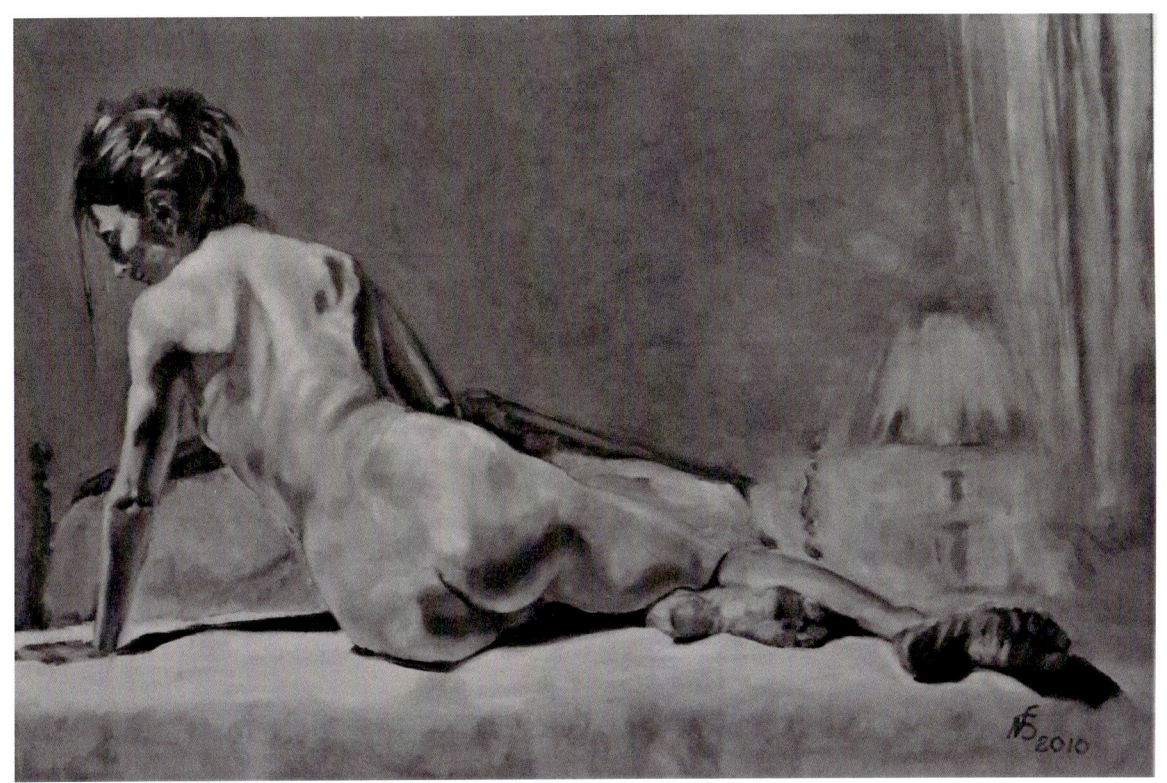

Female Nude Rising, 24" X 36", Oil on Canvas

 ## Understanding the Human Anatomy and Figure Drawing

The human body is not an easy subject to master. Learning its parts, its proportions, and mechanics of human movement can be challenging. I hope that you can be open minded and attempt to learn the human anatomy, as it will reward you when you apply your knowledge to artwork. In this book, the term "anatomy" is focused on the portrayal of forms and how body structures at different positions look.

Starting with Stick Figures

Being able to draw a stick figure tells me that you are aware of where things are located on the human body. It is important that you are aware of where the shoulder or knees or other joints on the body are located when drawing the figure. Being able to locate the various location points on the human body will create correct proportions for the figure that you are observing as shown.

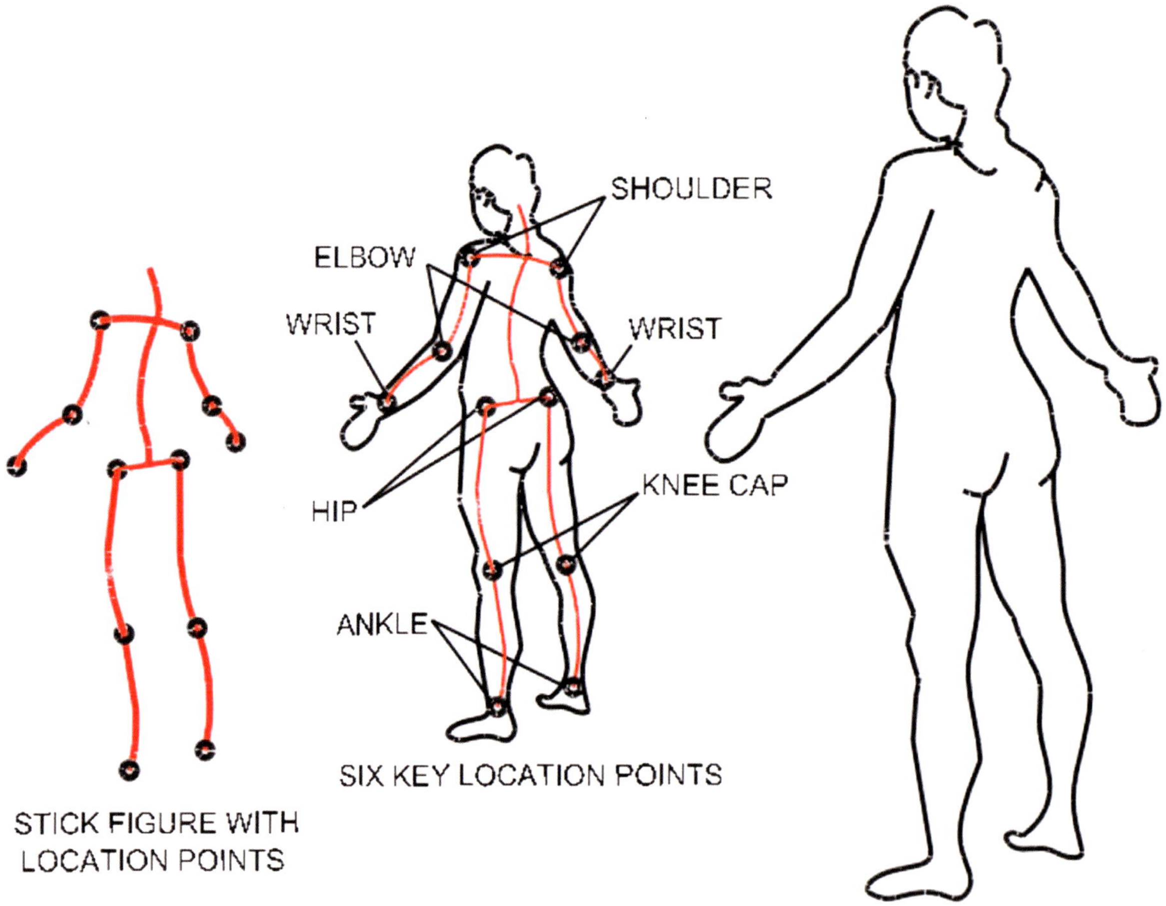

STICK FIGURE WITH
LOCATION POINTS

SIX KEY LOCATION POINTS

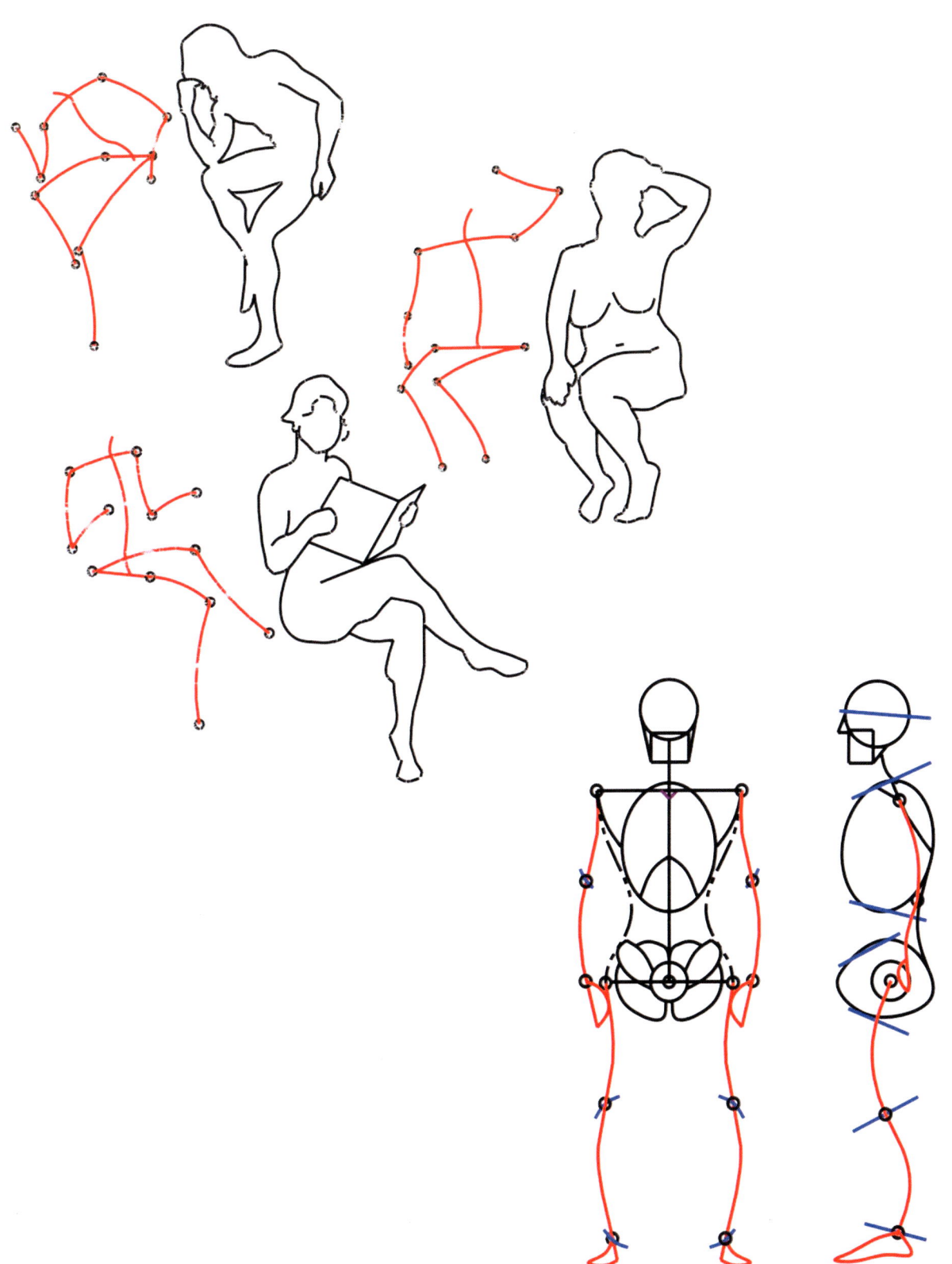

The Spine

The spine is curved and supports the body and allows movement of the torso. It consists of the **Cervical** (supports and provides mobility to the head), **Dorsal or Thoracic** (supports the ribs), and the **Lumbar** (a little before the pelvis, connected to the sacrum).

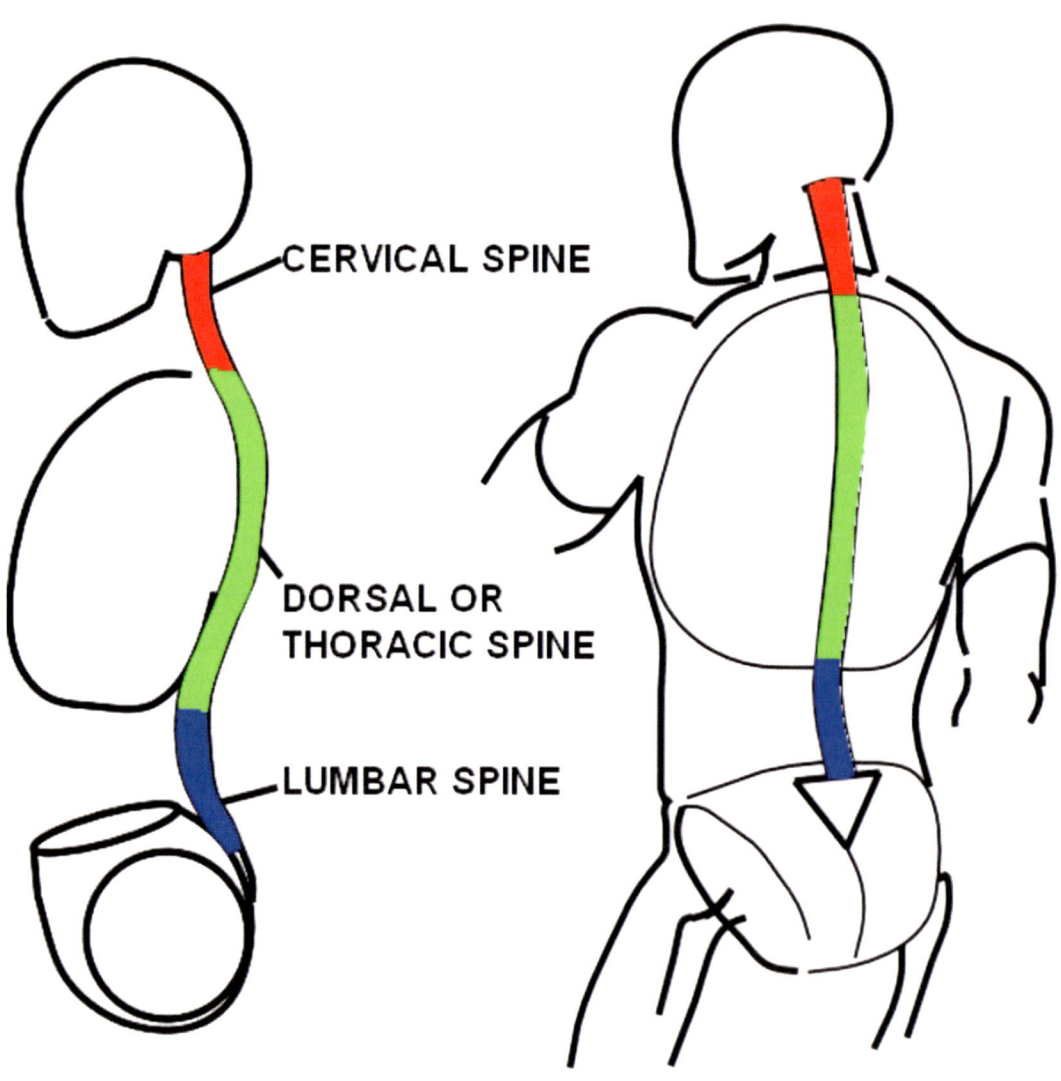

THE SPINE

The Neck

The neck has many muscles that move the head. The most visible muscle is the **sternocieidomastoid** that has a V-shape coming from the ear to the center of the clavicle's spine, surrounding the **Adam's apple** or **laryngeal prominence**. The Adam's apple is more protruding in men.

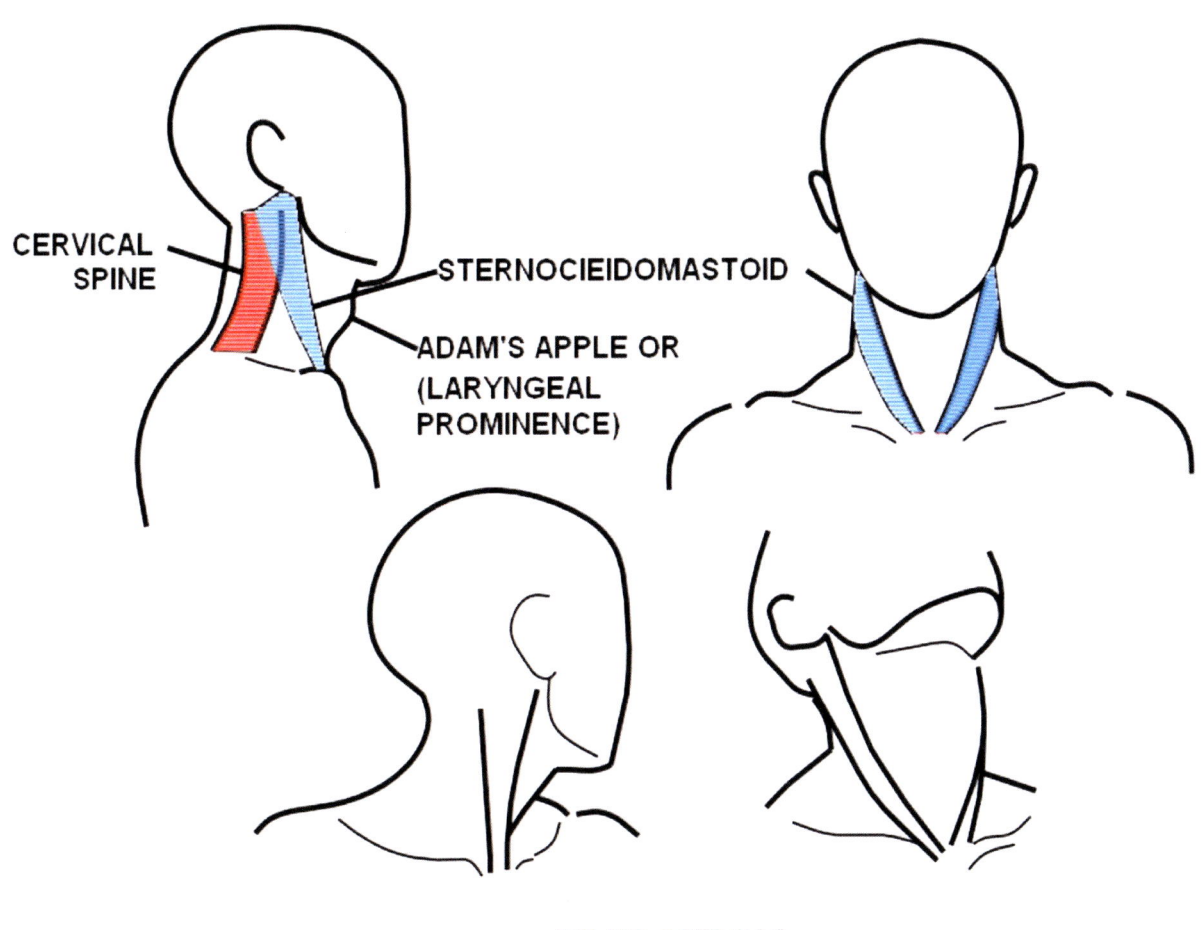

THE NECK

The Upper Body

As the cervical spine supports the head, the dorsal spine supports the rib cage. Many artists draw this area of the body as an oval shape resembling the **rib cage**. The **sternum** is in front and center of the rib cage. Artists create an imaginary line that divides the figure by using the sternum and spine as a guideline. The **clavicles** or **collarbone** are like bicycle handlebars. In the back, you will find the **scapulae** or **shoulder blades**. They are triangle shaped and help move the arms. The shape of the back changes following the movements of these bones.

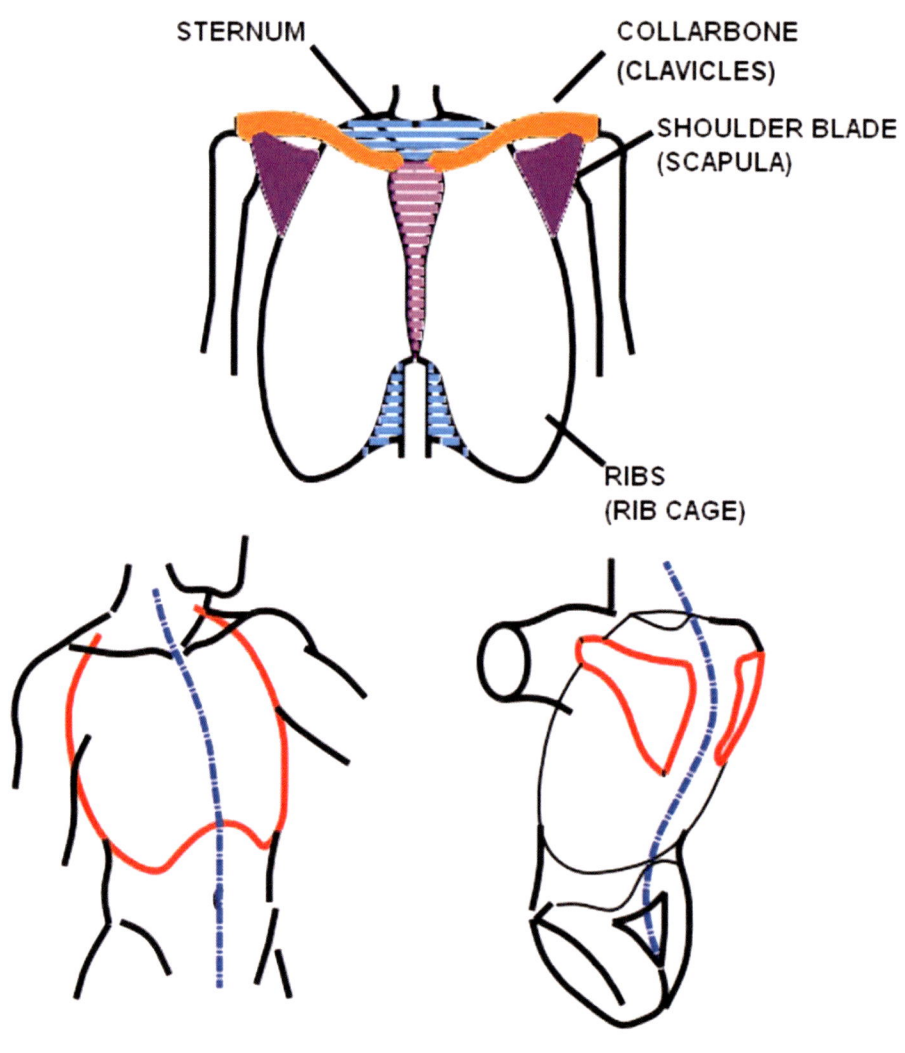

THE UPPER BODY

The Pelvis

The **Pelvis** is connected to the lumbar spine at the **sacrum**. The **ilium** is the pelvis hip's largest bone. Because the pelvis bones are irregular in shape, artists usually simplify them by drawing two discs for the ilium as a guide for drawing the angles of the hip and the sacrum as an inverted triangle. On the back, there are two dimples at the end of the spine before reaching the buttocks, which will help us to identify the location of the sacrum. Note that female hips are generally wider than male hips.

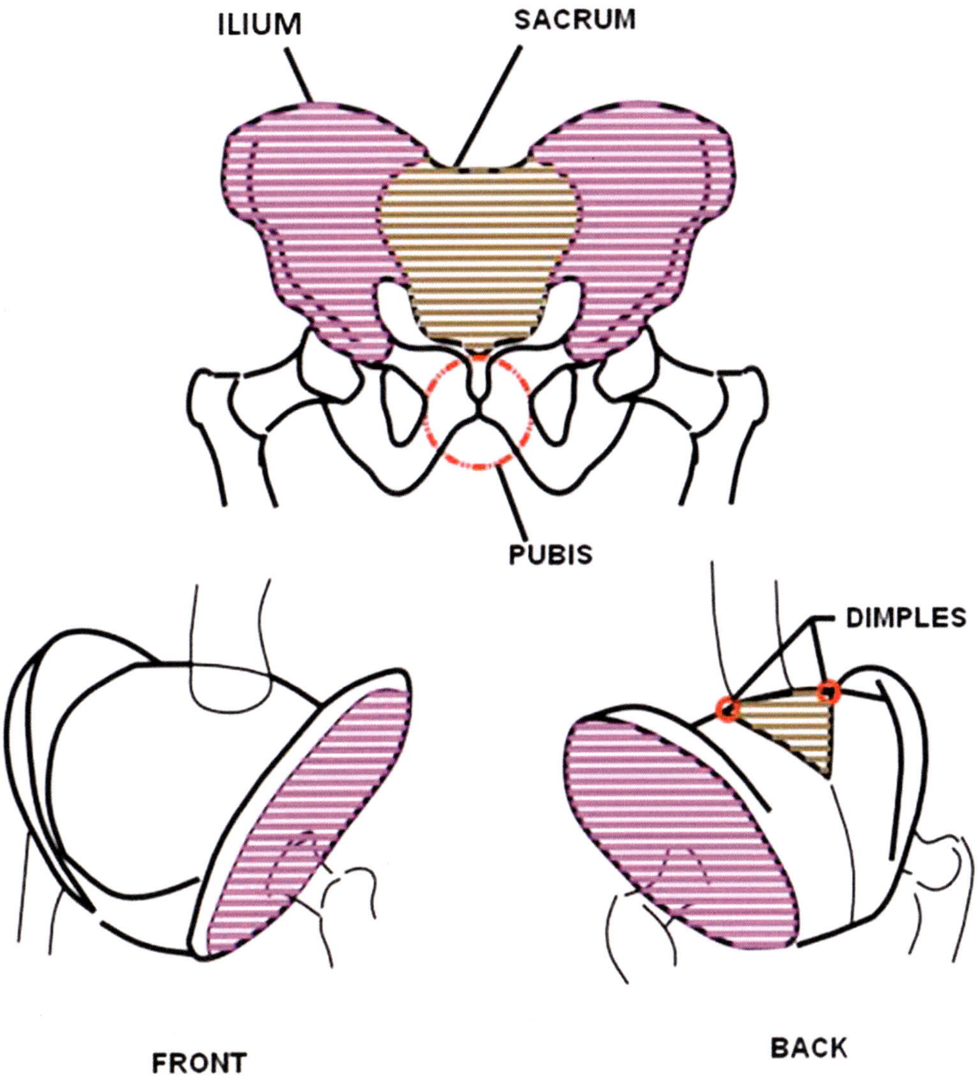

THE PELVIS

The Head Mass, Cage Mass, and Pelvis Mass

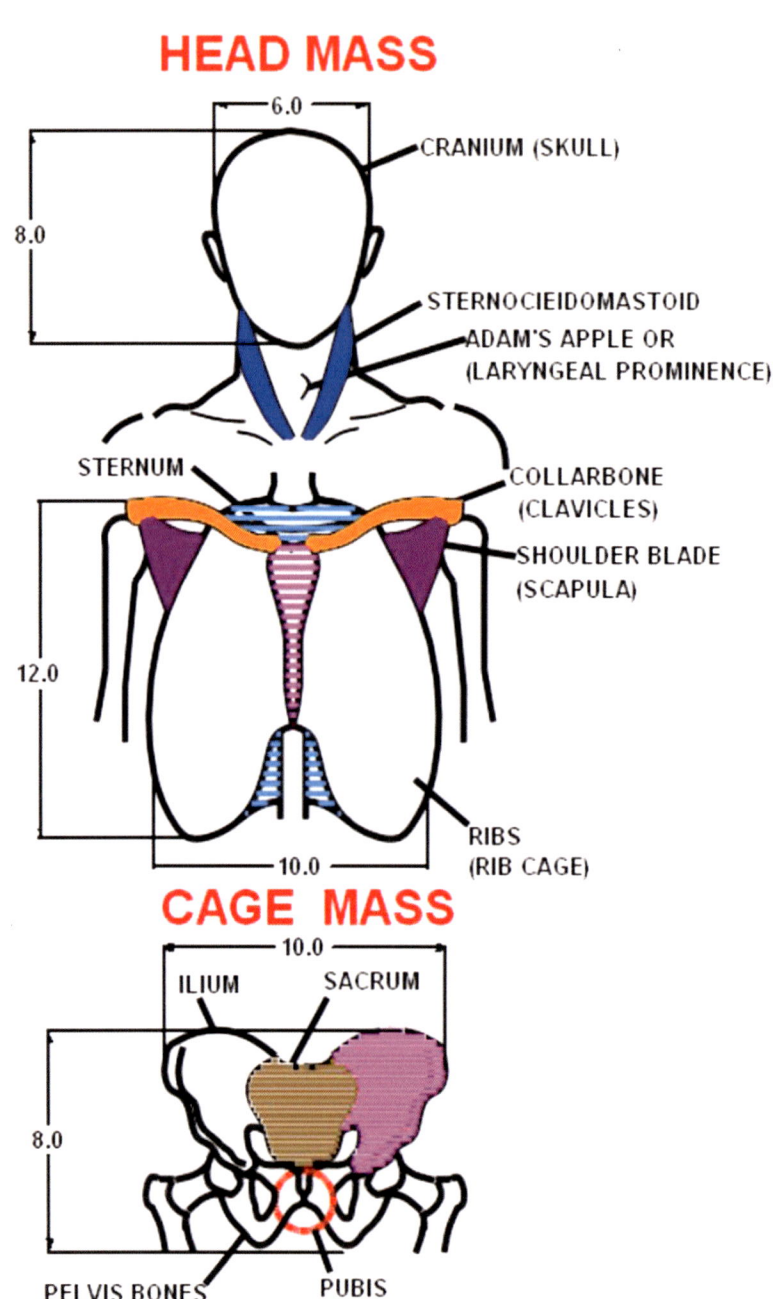

Limbs (Arms and Legs)

When it comes to understanding how to draw the **Limbs** of the body, we need to know how they can and cannot twist, bend and turn.

Arms

The **upper arm bone**, also known as the **humerus**, is a long bone that runs from the shoulder and scapula (shoulder blade) to the elbow. The **forearm** has two bones (the **radius laterally** and the **ulna medially**) and runs from the elbow to the wrist. These bones cross to allow the rotation of the wrist. Artists often use the wrist and the elbow as reference points to locate the orientation of the arm.

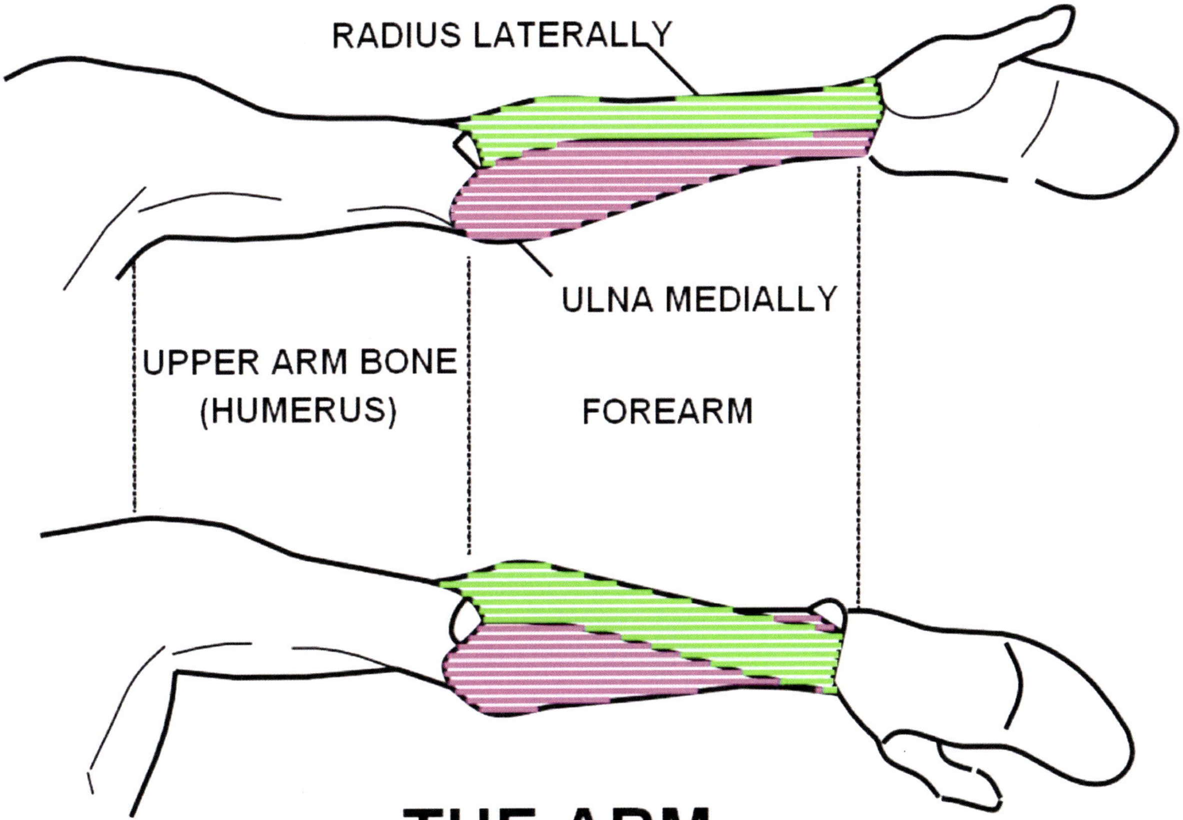

THE ARM

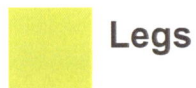 **Legs**

The legs consist of a few bones that the artist should be familiar with. The **femur**, located in the thigh; the **knee**, in the middle of the leg; and the **fibula** and the **tibia,** in the calf area. The artist should create a balanced figure, having the legs support the body. The legs must be balanced and have rhythm. Being slightly inclined in the femur from the hip to the knee, and the curves that create the contour of the leg, will put life into your figure drawings. When drawing the figure, the bones of the ankle are placed at different heights, with the fibula on the outer side being lower.

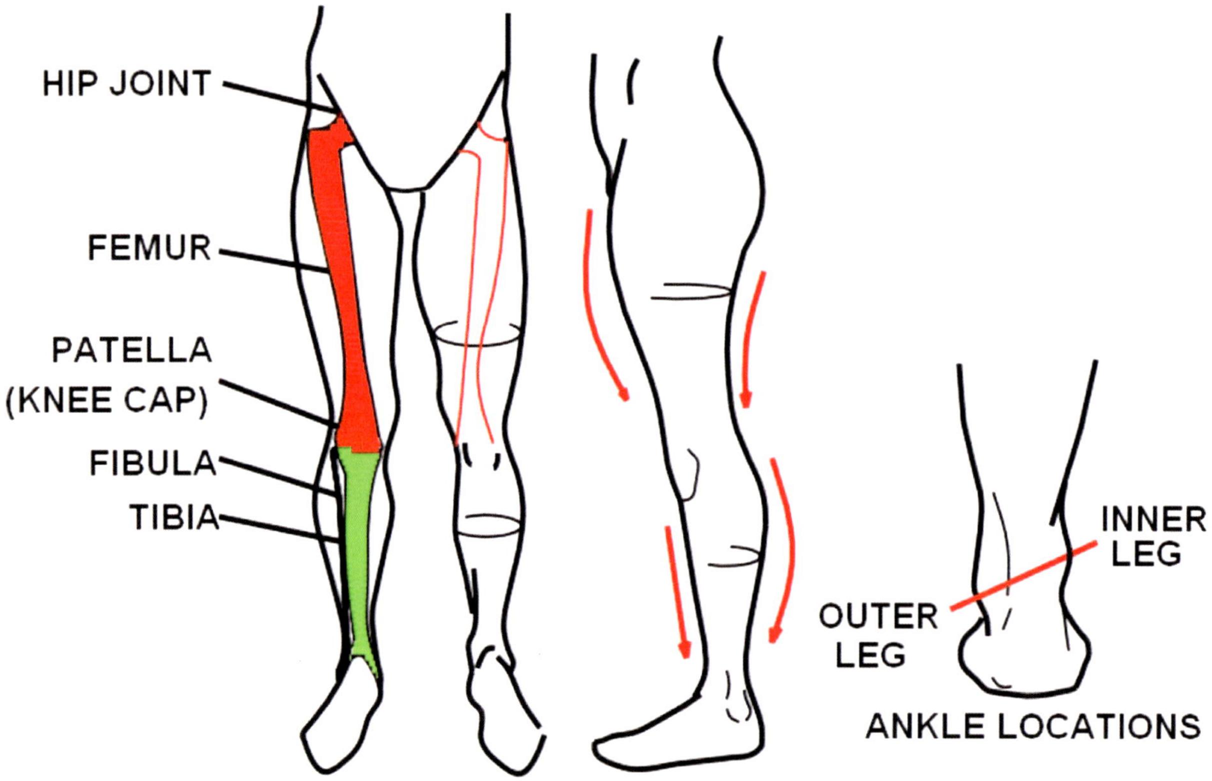

THE LEGS

Proportions

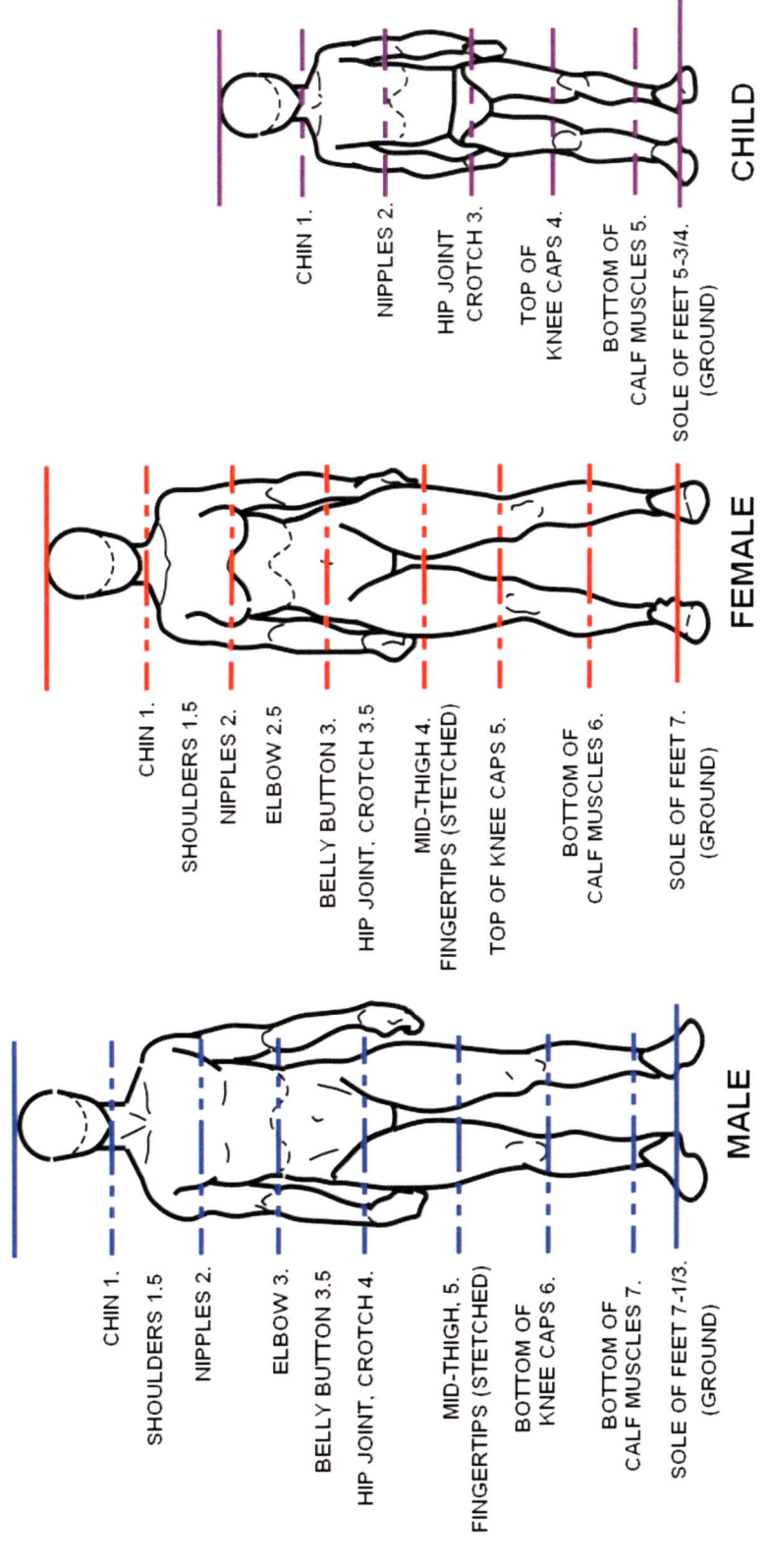

 **Drawing the Human Figure**

When it comes to learning how to draw the human figure, understanding the structures of the human anatomy will help in creating realistic human figures. Artist's anatomy can feel overwhelming at first, but you only have to learn a fraction of the anatomy terminology that would be required of a medical student. Start with the basic shapes and as they get more complex, you will see your human figure take on a sense of form. Understanding the human figure's muscles and how they change will give the human figure a realistic illusion of 3-dimensional form.

Understanding the muscles of the human figure doesn't mean that you should exaggerate them, unless you want these muscles to be the focal point. Artists most likely want to depict the human figure by showing what the human figure is doing (some action or emotion), and will use knowledge of anatomy to reinforce that statement. Draw the human figure by observing its unique shapes. People have different body shapes. You have to look at your human figure, observe and adapt, and determine what shapes best fit your human figure.

Recreate what you see by using your observational skills of what is important to you. This means that you are not copying by recreating the human figure in your artwork. You will learn to combine your knowledge of anatomy forms to develop volume and create something original. Artists should not just replicate what is before them, but should interpret what they understand and bring that knowledge into the artwork.

Proportion, anatomy and having good observational skills are important. But these are not what makes an interesting figure drawing. The artist must learn to create a dynamic and interesting flair to the drawing. This requires you to learn to draw a little more freely. Your drawing should show energy and attitude. It is acceptable to even exaggerate or distort in your drawing if you do so intentionally.

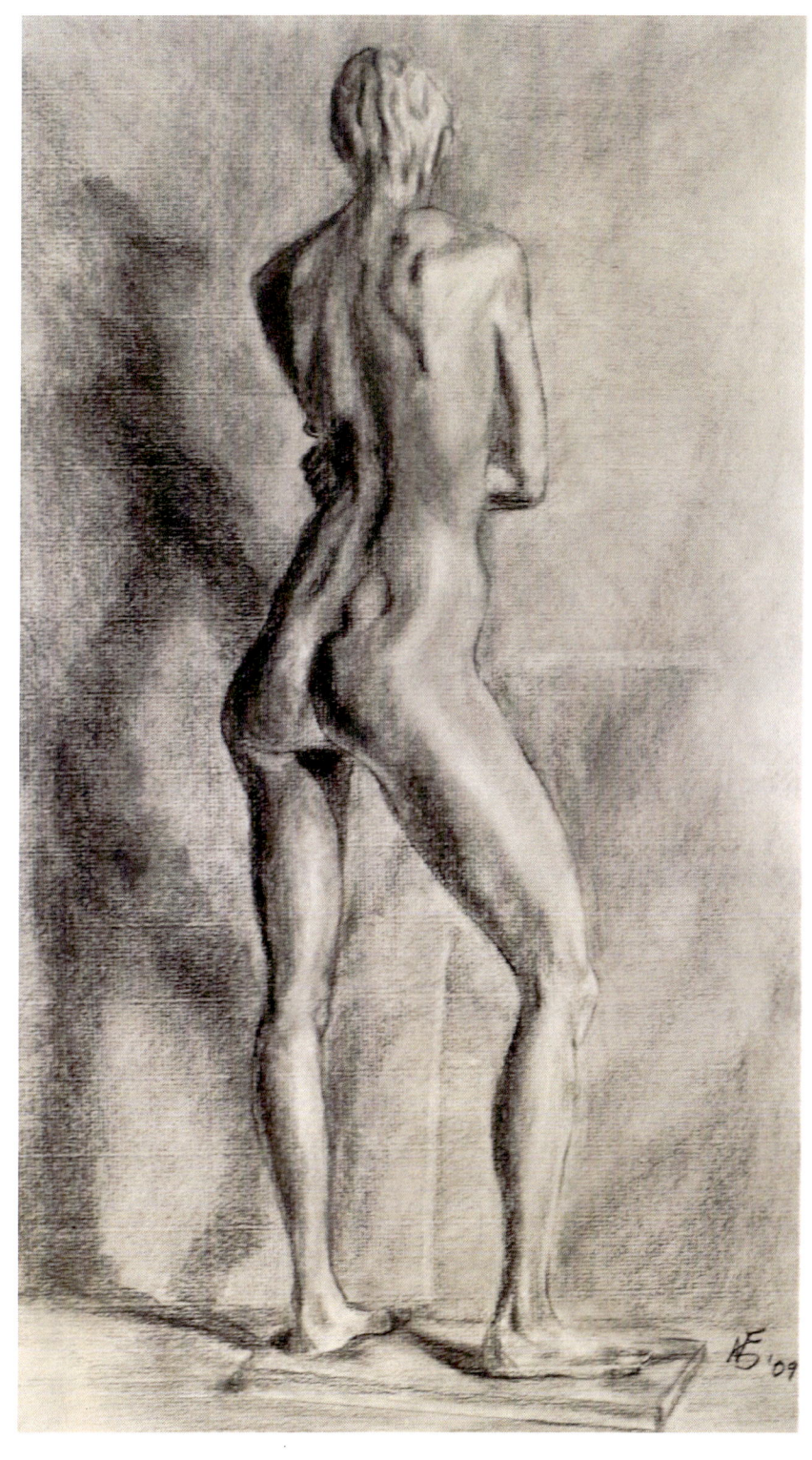

Mia, Rear Figure Study, 21" X 12", Charcoal on Charcoal Paper,

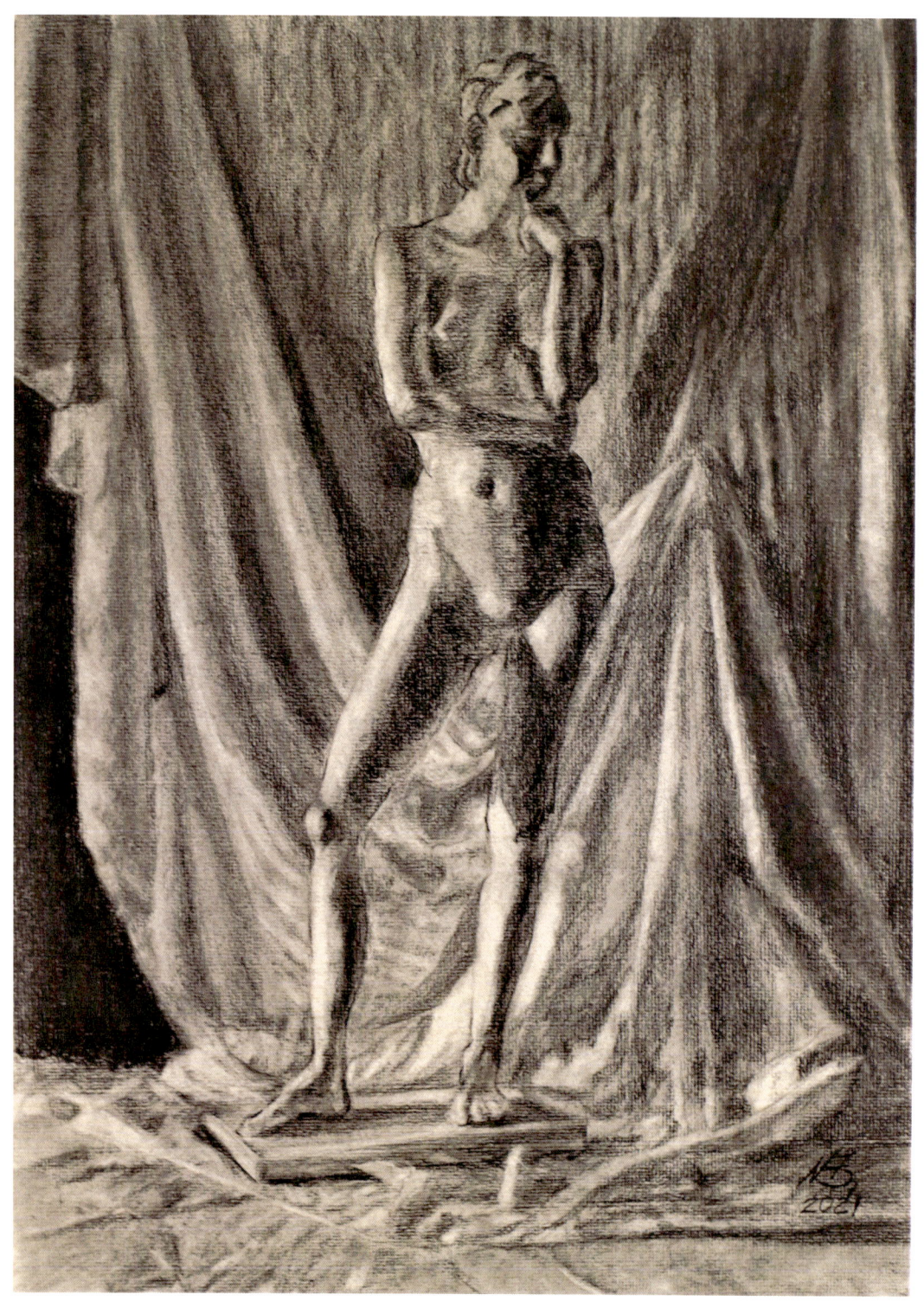

Surrounded by Drapery, 22" X 16", Charcoal on Charcoal Paper

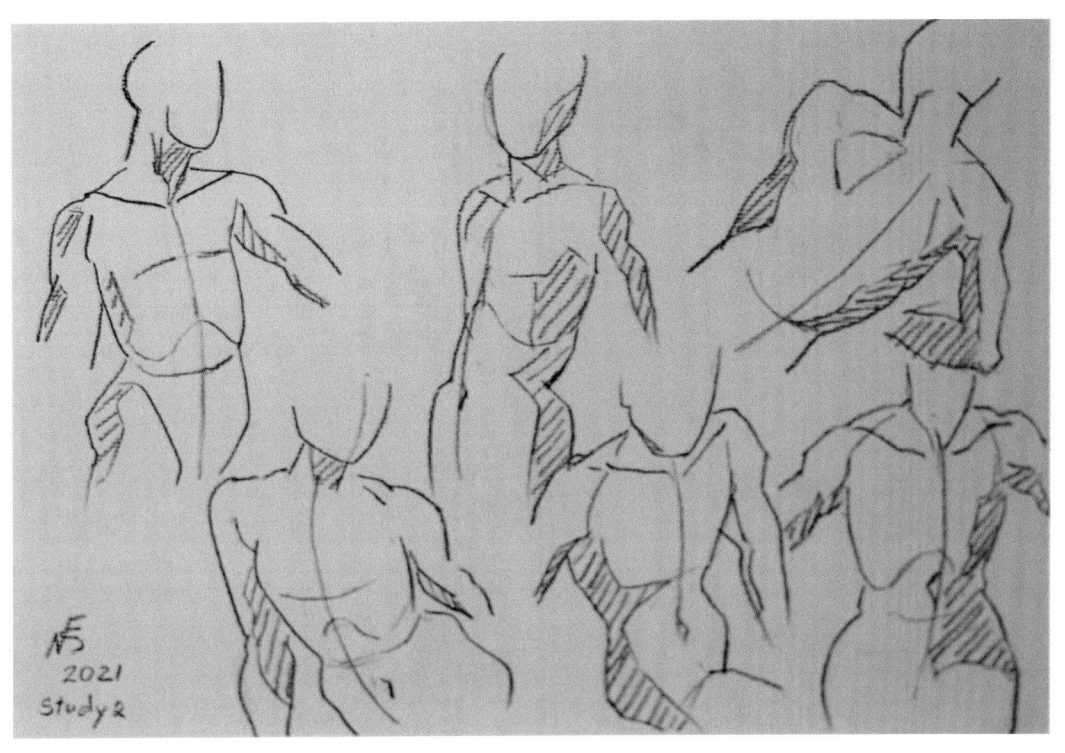

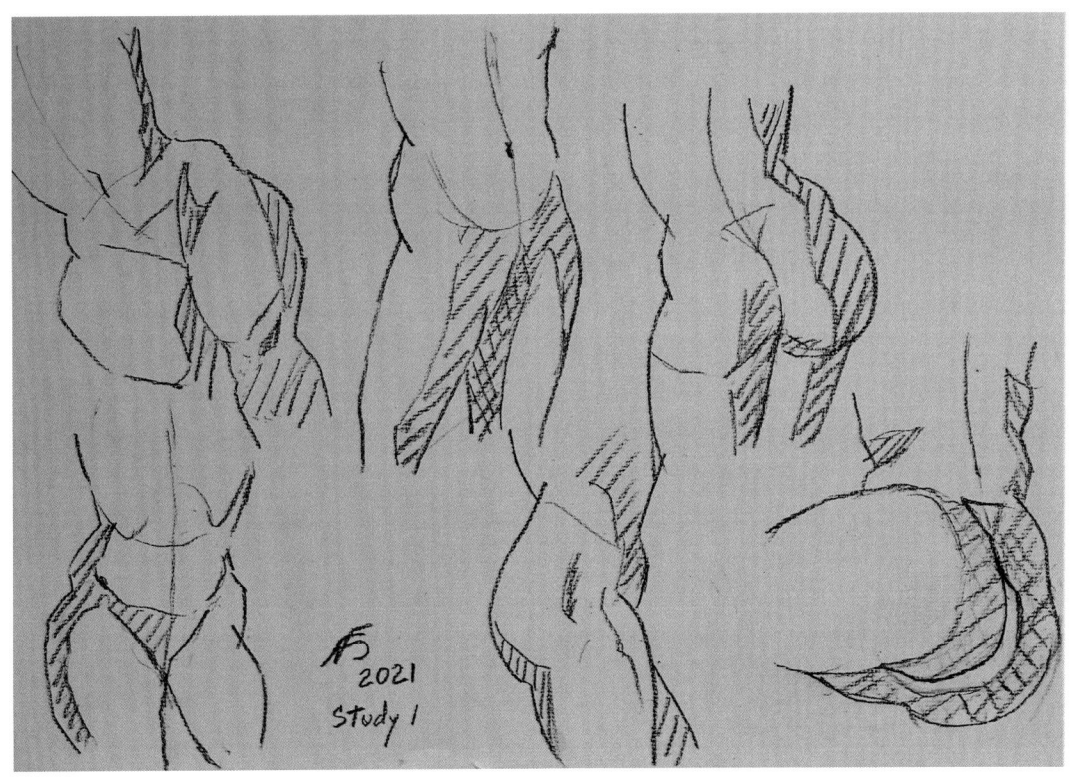

48

# Learning to be Disciplined in Learning Art

Most of us do not have the luxury or finances to go to the top art school to learn how to draw and paint. So, these "Introduction to Drawing" series of books were designed to aid your knowledge and skills as a guide to being self-taught because they introduce you to some basic, but important, concepts. As a self-taught artist, you can become a great artist provided you are disciplined. We have many master artists who have been self-taught, so you won't be alone in working to master your skills in becoming an artist.

In becoming a better artist, you will have to be able to look at and judge your art in an unbiased and critical manner. Always look for areas where you can improve on. Don't expect to create a masterpiece, but always thrive to do so. Learn from the masters by copying their work, in order to understand how they achieved their masterpieces. Still, it is important that you discover your own style. To become successful, you have to practice, practice, and more practice. In other words, you have to put in the time studying and doing. You must not procrastinate. You must work on your artworks and dedicate yourself to a time to do this work. Look at professionals for inspiration, but do not compare yourself to them. You are the only thing you should be focusing on. Try to keep and document your work. This will help you see your improvement from earlier works. Take part in community art competitions, exhibitions, and art demonstrations.

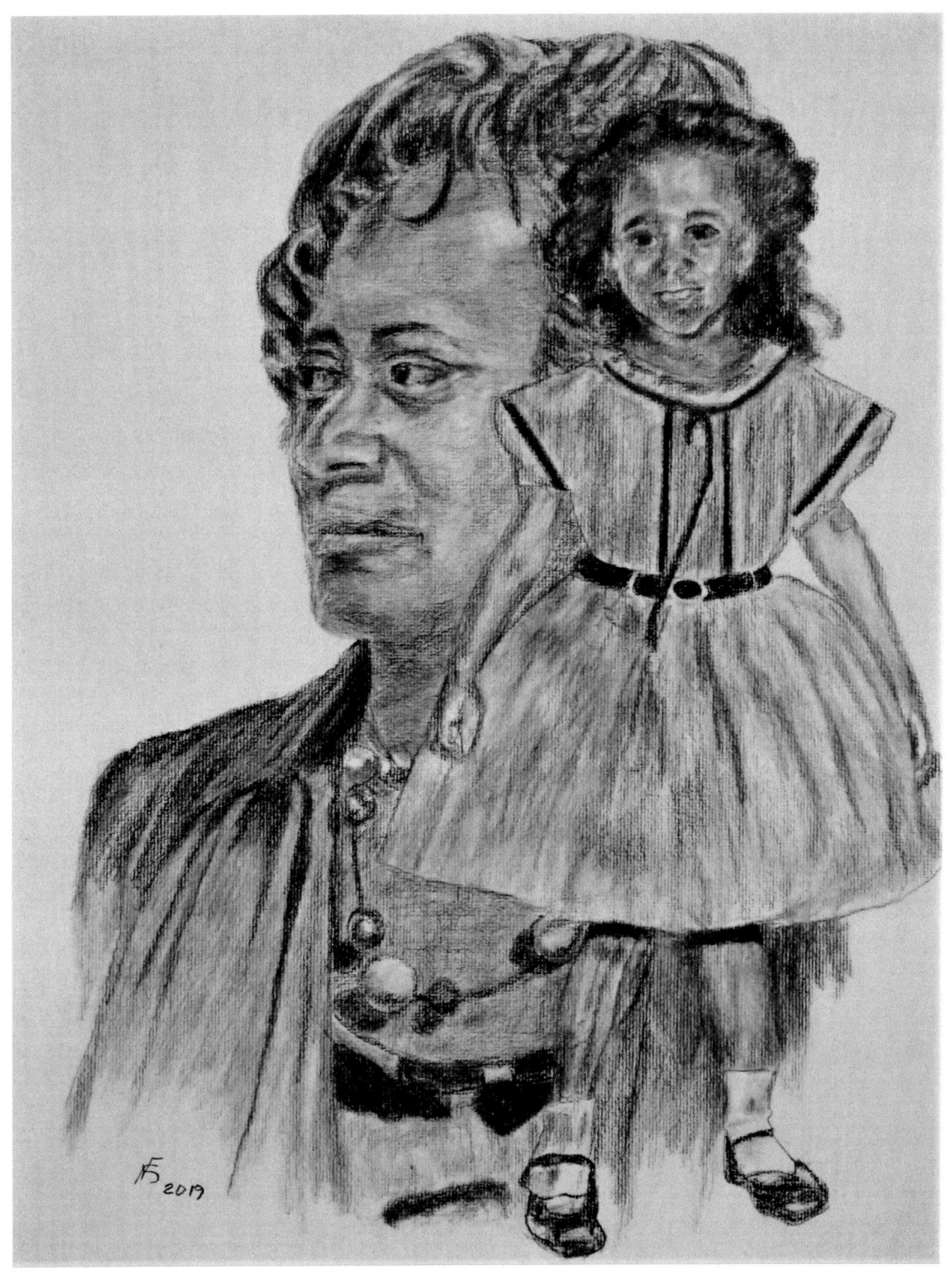

Kind Hearted, 16" X 20", Charcoal on Charcoal Paper

The Charcoal Summary

In this book, we explored the various types of charcoal: the willow (vine) charcoal sticks which are soft and great for creating free flowing lines and blending; the charcoal pencils that come in a variety of hardness; and the white pastel (white charcoal) used in combination with black charcoal to create highlights on toned paper. The ideal paper is one that has a tooth (rough texture) the charcoal is able to grip to.

Charcoal is a little fragile, so in order to sharpen and shape the ends, you should use a utility knife and fine-tooth sandpaper block to sharpen your charcoal pencils and sticks. Be careful. When sharpening with these very sharp blades, carefully slide the utility knife away from yourself along the charcoal willow (vine) or pencils ends. Protect your drawing from smudging by placing a piece of paper between your hands and your artwork paper, or wear a cotton glove while you are working. Remember that your hands contain oils on them and oils are not your friend when it comes to your artwork.

Students will often blend charcoal using their fingers, but I suggest using a stump, tortillon, paintbrushes, or rag to spread and blend your charcoal. Experiment with these different items for each will create a different effect. Not just with a charcoal drawing, you should step away from your artwork to look at it from a distance. This will help you view the art from a different perspective. You will better see how your viewers will experience the artwork.

Remember in whatever medium you use, start out light and build up to the darker tones. It is easy to make darker tones than to lighten them. The kneaded eraser is not only able to remove mistakes, but also to add highlights, draw, and add textures by removing charcoal from various areas of the artwork. Finally, protect your artwork from getting damaged. You have worked hard, so place your artwork in a secured place away from dampness and sunlight. You may want to store your artwork in a portfolio or place the artwork in a frame.

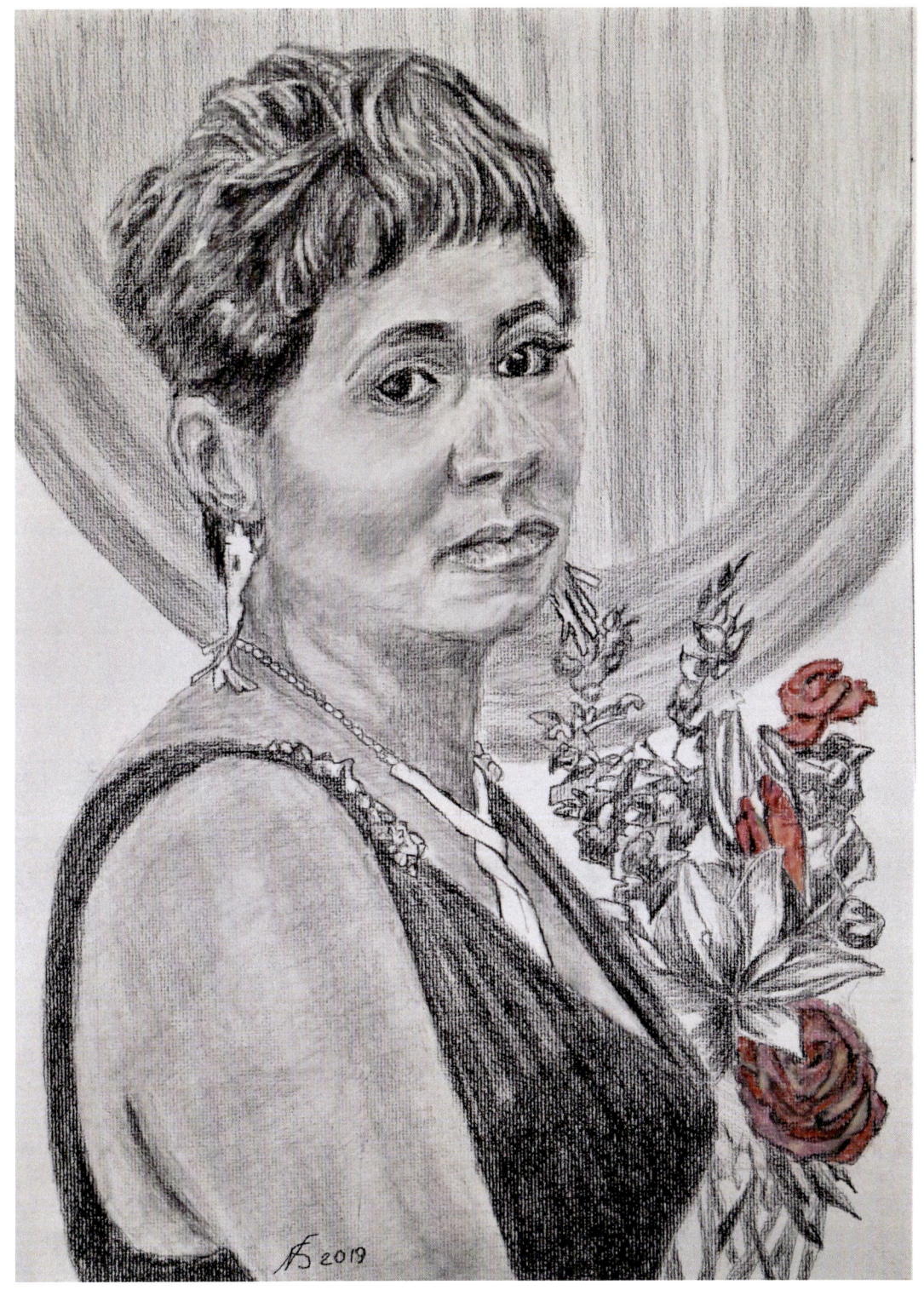

Cupcake, 16" X 20", Charcoal on Charcoal Paper

www.ingramcontent.com/pod-product-compliance
Lightning Source LLC
Chambersburg PA
CBRC100912220526
45473CB00010B/2867